PRAISE

"Recruiting for leadership roles is probably the most important action most organizations ever take, and they are often flying blind. Simon Mullins and David Lord, two of the world's experts on this topic, offer real insights as well as a practical guide to running the leadership recruiting process."
—Peter Cappelli, Professor of Management, The Wharton School

"Talent is the lifeblood of all great organizations. David and Simon have created an invaluable resource for organizations seeking to find the right people for the challenges of the future. Their unique approach and wealth of expertise makes this book a must-read for leaders wishing to up their talent game."
—Lisa Brummel, former Chief People Officer, Microsoft, and Owner of WNBA Champions Seattle Storm

"Attracting and retaining the right leaders is key to the success of any organization. This book artfully captures 25-plus years of learnings in the field, providing a valuable practical guide for human resources leaders to improve their approach to executive recruiting."
—Peter Fasolo, Executive Vice President & Chief Human Resources Officer, Johnson & Johnson

"Talent Acquisition leaders have many hats to wear. When it comes to leadership recruiting, this is your guide."
—Aditya Singh, Worldwide Director, Global Talent Acquisition, Colgate-Palmolive

"Whether you're a corporate talent leader looking to start up a leadership recruiting function, or thinking about how to take your team to the next level, this book has the advice you need."
—Amy Goldfinger, Senior Vice President, Talent, Walmart

"Finding the right talent has never been more important, and nowhere is this more critical than at the top. This book, by leading experts in the field, is an outstanding summary of the challenges and opportunities in this area, and will no doubt help data-driven professionals elevate their game."
—Tomas Chamorro-Premuzic, Professor of Business Psychology at Columbia and University College London

LEADERSHIP RECRUITING

STRATEGY, TACTICS AND TOOLS
FOR HIRING ORGANIZATIONS

SIMON MULLINS + DAVID LORD

LEADERSHIP RECRUITING
Strategy, Tactics and Tools for Hiring Organizations

Copyright ® 2020 LDRS Publishing, Inc.
www.LDRSPublishing.com

ISBN: 978-0-578-77591-3
Library of Congress Control Number: 2020919914

Printed in the United States of America.

Edited by: Monica Jainschigg
Cover Design: Jayme Johnson, Worthy Marketing Group
Interior Layout: Jayme Johnson, Worthy Marketing Group
Book Development & Marketing: Carolyn Monaco, Monaco Associates

CONTENTS
• • •

LEADERSHIP RECRUITING

PREFACE
• • •

How to develop leaders is a well-covered topic. How to recruit them at senior levels remains more of a mystery. *Leadership Recruiting* aims to correct that with independent information and advice that will help hiring organizations address ineffective behavior in this vital activity.

These insights come straight from the horse's mouth—from those who have led executive recruiting at many of the world's leading organizations. Even the best of them would admit that they have room to improve, but they have many lessons learned, which we share with you here.

Amid unprecedented, unanticipated, and—in some cases—existential challenges, today's organizations have an opportunity to reevaluate their approach to every function, talent being a primary concern in both human and business terms. CEOs and HR leaders are taking a hard look at senior management capabilities, as well as gaps in those capabilities.

While many organizations can adapt existing management structures to new business realities, the emphasis has changed. Leadership skills that were right for 2019 are not the same for the 2020s. The initial work is falling on Talent Management and Development, but once current management has been realigned, the focus will quickly move to leadership recruiting.

What follows is a case for leadership recruiting management and how to do it. The good news is, it will help you save money now and help you make smart investments for the future.

The process we describe here is scalable. You may be a startup fazed (or not) by new realities, reevaluating plans and the people needed to carry them out. Or you may be a Global 100 and dealing with these issues by the boatload. But the same questions matter: What is the right track for recruiting key people for your organization at a critical time? What are best approaches and tools?

If you're looking for a page-turner, this is not it. It's more of a page-stopper. The idea is to see where you fit into the plot, to pause at every relevant page and to use it to inform next steps. Whether you dive into the relevant sections or read it cover to cover (and we hope you do) Leadership Recruiting is the reference book for any organization leader looking for the best possible independent information on how to recruit at the top of the house.

INTRODUCTION
• • •

L eadership recruiting lives at the intersection of corporate strategy and people. Here, the toughest decisions are made on who will shape the future of the enterprise. You might say it's the most interesting, vital, challenging, and sometimes downright exciting place to be in an organization.

Leadership recruiting is nearly impossible to quantify—and has forever resisted management. Inevitably, however, because of its importance, big advancements are being made on how to do it well. That's what this handbook is about.

We will examine the development of the corporate executive search management function, the process of finding and recruiting leaders, how to select and engage executive search consultants, how to assess candidates, and how to recruit directly at the executive level, as well as numerous subtopics under those umbrellas. In addition, we'll provide tools and templates to use in implementing this knowledge.

Together, we the authors have explored the world of corporate executive recruiting for more than two decades, starting in 1996 with the formation of the Executive Search Information Exchange (ESIX). In October of that year, IBM invited nine other leading companies to an initial meeting, and since then, ESIX has grown to comprise more than 90 organizations worldwide, has met more than 400 times, and today operates as a global resource on executive search for hiring organizations.

The idea is that there is value in:
- The strategic management of corporate executive recruiting
- Building a community of top practitioners sharing experiences
- Developing better information and tools
- Creating a greater flow of leadership talent information

These conversations among corporate executive recruiting leaders, including presentations by practitioners and consultants, annual surveys, and ongoing research, form the base of knowledge from which the information presented here is drawn. Participation in ESIX is for hiring organizations only—done independent of the interests of executive search consultants and others who sell services to corporations—and is the viewpoint of what's recommended here.

ESIX also operates the Executive Search Academy, where corporate executive recruiting and human resources executives advance their understanding of what works, based on the experiences of hundreds of large organizations over many years. *Leadership Recruiting* captures the highlights of these learnings.

We welcome your comments and insights as we continue to advance best practices to a point where the most important hiring decisions are made with the greatest opportunity for success.

1.

THE CORPORATE EXECUTIVE SEARCH INITIATIVE
• • •

A BRIEF HISTORY OF EXECUTIVE RECRUITING

Leaders have recruited direct reports since the beginning of civilization. But the practice of systematically identifying and attracting key executives is only about 100 years old and came about when management consultants included executive search in their offerings.

"Often, the best solution to a management problem is the right person," said Edwin Booz, founder of the great management consulting firm Booz Allen Hamilton, in 1918. Some of Booz's first consulting engagements were executive searches for growing companies in the Chicago area: Montgomery Ward, Marshall Field & Co., and the Bank of Winnetka.

After World War II, with wartime experience that could be applied to economic expansion (for example, the Whiz Kids—a group of World War II veterans who became Ford Motor Co. executives), management consulting became a big deal. Booz Allen and McKinsey & Co. grew into global firms, with important executive search capabilities. In fact, Booz Allen became … let's call it the greatest search firm of all time, establishing methods and professional practices and employing consultants who later became founders of several of today's largest executive search firms.

But during rapid growth in the 1960s, Booz Allen found that it had too many management consulting clients that were off-limits to its search practice. The need to avoid conflicts with their larger management consulting practices prompted key partners in the search practice to leave.

From Booz Allen came Spencer Stuart (the man and the firm, which later spawned Egon Zehnder International), Gardner Heidrick, Sidney Boyden, Bob Lamalie, and others who went on to found firms that led the field and, in some cases, continue to do so. Search practice leaders Ward Howell and Jack Handy left McKinsey to start Ward Howell International and Handy Associates, both leading players at one time.

By the end of the 1980s, nearly all of the management consulting firms were out of the executive search business. Yet to this day, search firms with these origins still consider themselves to be management consultants focused on executive search. It's an important distinction from the specialty shops of the recruiting business, whose strength is not management advice, but information on who's who in a particular industry or function and how to get to them.

Accounting firms and their Management Advisory Services provided another platform for assisting clients in finding executive leaders. Like the management consultants, they addressed leadership needs (especially in the finance function) and developed search practices of a similar size and caliber as the consulting firms. Sure enough, around 1970, the accounting firms too began an exit from executive search for the same reason as management consultants: The firms' search consultants were too restricted by accounting/consulting client relationships that blocked executives from those companies from being recruited.

Lester Korn and Richard Ferry left Peat Marwick to form Korn Ferry. (Interestingly, Korn Ferry originally charged for services on a time-and-expense basis, as was the norm in accounting and consulting. Only later did they switch to the more profitable fee structure based on a percentage of the hired executive's compensation.) And upon leaving Price Waterhouse, William H. Clark launched a firm that included Russell Reynolds, who went on to form the firm that still bears his name.

Along with the spinoffs from consulting and accounting firms, specialty retained executive search firms ("retained" on an exclusive basis to recruit for a specific position on behalf of a specific client) sprang up to serve every major industry and function. The first of these firms in the US was founded in 1926 by Thorndike Deland, an expert in recruiting buyers for big department stores in New York and Boston, including the May Co. and Filene's. Thousands of small firms followed—both generalists, who took pride in their process, and specialists, who sold engagements because they already knew "everybody."

Meanwhile, local search firms emerged in Europe, and during the 1960s, the largest US firms opened offices there. Today, retained executive search is a US$18 billion business worldwide and an almost universally accepted tool for senior management recruiting.

FROM CONSULTING TO A CORPORATE PERSPECTIVE

Not every organization has used search firms to find its next generation of leaders. Indeed, most have done it themselves, with varied outcomes. CEOs and other senior executives often use their own networks to identify and recruit candidates. Some have relied on advertising (and these days, social media). These informal practices dominated the process for decades. Engaging search consultants remained a small part of the overall picture until it reached critical mass in the 1980s and gained acceptance as a standard way of doing business.

At the same time, companies began to look at the corporate function more carefully. In 1980, at Chase Manhattan Bank in New York, J. Gregory Coleman launched what may have been the first corporate in-house executive search function. It was a sign that corporations were beginning to consider a more disciplined approach to hiring leaders. And in the early 1990s, when reengineering became a business trend, studies began to show that large companies were spending big money—several million dollars a year, and sometimes much more—on executive search services that were often successful, but often not.

Given the function's importance beyond the search fees themselves, corporate initiatives to improve these outcomes took hold. This line of thinking got a boost when, in 1998, McKinsey published its War for Talent research. The study highlighted demographics showing an upcoming shortage of executive-level talent, demonstrated the high stakes of competing for it, and offered "talent imperatives" for addressing the challenge. These imperatives included instilling a talent mindset in the organization, creating extreme employee value propositions, building a high-performance culture, developing talent, making room for talent, and retaining talent.

What set the study apart from others was this recommendation: Recruit great talent at the executive level.

Until then, conventional wisdom had suggested that executive recruiting was a necessary evil. At GE, CEO Jack Welch famously said that any use of executive search at his company was done to make up for mistakes made in management development. Leaders at IBM, HP, Procter & Gamble, and many other companies had shared that view.

But now McKinsey had offered authoritative research showing that executive recruiting was not a necessary evil, but a strategic opportunity. It put things in a whole new light. Companies noticed and, one by one, created the in-house function of executive recruiting management. They began to fill those roles with professionals who understood executive recruiting, often taking consultants from search firms to run the corporate initiative.

The work and growth of the Executive Search Information Exchange (ESIX) has reflected this trend. Today, having an executive search management function is the norm for any large organization, and an advantage for smaller ones that have needs worthy of oversight.

WHAT WE'RE UP AGAINST

Just in case this sounds eminently doable, it's important to underscore the high failure rate of unmanaged search activity (40%) and note a few bad habits of corporations that don't take search management seriously. Veteran search consultant Jay Gaines calls this the "leadership paradox": Why is what's most important often least successful?

Too often, at too many companies, hiring is treated as the province of the executive in charge rather than of the enterprise, Gaines says. As a result, little learning is shared within the organization.

We might add that this can have more ramifications than you might imagine. When individual hiring executives build relationships with search consultants, they may have their own agendas in mind rather than those of the enterprise—which may even include their own career ambitions. Furthermore, at too many companies, standardized hiring processes are formalities rather than strategic tools. And too many hiring managers believe, but cannot substantiate, that they are good at selecting people and building teams. Finally, Gaines says, companies often fail at integrating new hires, either tying the hands of new leaders or urging them to take action before they understand or establish the level of trust needed to make big changes.

He offers the following remedies:
- Recognize how critical it is to do this right. Systematize interviewing and integration.
- Grasp the values, competencies, and personalities that propel

your organization, then hire to match.
- Acknowledge risk in senior-level hiring. Analyze failures and look for patterns.
- Encourage candor and truth in interviewing. Tell candidates what's really going on.
- Make successful hiring, integration, development, and objective evaluation a priority for which every hiring executive is held accountable. If you can do only one thing, this is it.
- Manage to the long term, as if executive hiring were like investing for returns over time.
- Architect the integration of new hires: Allow six months to learn; two years to measurable impact.
- Be prepared to acknowledge hiring mistakes. They will happen—just don't ignore or fail to learn from them.
- Embrace and nurture talent you already have. Stretch people to the limits of their capabilities.
- Attend to the strength of the middle ranks. Hire and experiment for long-term payback.

THE CASE FOR MANAGING SEARCH ACTIVITY

Any organization that really cares about being successful must continuously pay attention to how well it manages executive recruiting. Yes, the development of leaders is even more important. But talent-focused companies always have some executive-level needs that can't be filled from the inside. And, given that failure rates of recruited executives are higher than those of promoted ones, sound management of search activity is vital.

Working with hundreds of Fortune 500 companies over the last 25 years, we have found that ineffective management of search activity is responsible for most failed searches. When there's no oversight of search activity, four out of 10 searches fail—and even the successful ones take an average of six months to complete. Search firms aren't perfect, but the better ones deliver qualified candidates in a timely manner 80%–90% of the time. Corporations, on the other hand, cancel or fail to complete searches 20%–30% of the time, when no one's overseeing the effort.

Reasons for failure by the hiring organization include: not being clear on the need; not having consensus; changing one's mind; creating the appearance of a search without intending to complete it; failing to sell the position to top candidates and/or losing them to competing offers; failing to impress leading candidates with a process that shows the organization knows what it's doing. Some search cancellations are the inevitable result of restructurings and changes in business conditions that are beyond control. But most cancellations or failures can be prevented.

Our research shows that companies that actively manage search activity can cut failures in half and reach overall completion rates of 80% or more. And they can reduce average cycle time from six months to four months, or less in some cases.

The business case for management of search activities at large corporations is powerful. Let's say your organization is going to initiate 30 executive searches this year for positions averaging US$300K in compensation. An executive at that level is making a contribution to the organization's bottom line of some multiple of their pay. That multiple will vary greatly—and we don't really know what it is—but we can imagine that on average it's at least twice what the person is being paid; more likely three times or sometimes much more.

Let's say it's only twice the person's pay. So on average, a US$300K executive is contributing US$600K, in some fashion, to the organization's revenues. If we initiate 30 searches without oversight, it's likely that 12 will fail. With oversight, only six will fail (we have years of survey work to support this finding). That's six executives on board this year contributing US$3.6 million to the bottom line, from positions that otherwise would have gone unfilled. In addition, by reducing cycle time from six months to four months, the organization earns an additional US$2.4 million in revenues, if you will, from getting its 24 newly hired executives on the job two months more quickly. And, by the way (assuming we've been using search firms), we're saving US$600K in search fees by cutting our failure rate in half.

That's a big payoff—US$6.6 million—for a modest investment in a Director of Executive Recruiting.

PREFERRED-PROVIDER PROGRAMS

Starting in the 1980s, corporate management of executive search activity began to take the form of "preferred-provider programs" (PPPs)—a method of organizing executive search activity in the hands of a selected group of search firms. The idea was to reduce costs and improve service by developing stronger relationships with a smaller number of search firms. Up to this point, most hiring managers considered it their prerogative to engage a search firm of their choice under whatever terms the search firm set. Now, hiring managers had to listen to corporate heads of procurement who had gained a hand in managing search firm costs and therefore the selection of providers.

In a typical preferred-provider program, the director of executive recruiting:

- Gathers information on the organization's use of search to date
- Designs a program for selecting search partners
- Develops standard terms of engagement
- Reviews the performance of known and new search consultants
- Selects "best-at" consultants for expected needs
- Executes one-year relationship agreements
- Reviews performance regularly

PPPs continue to be popular, but they have not enjoyed unqualified success. Some have failed their organizations, for three main reasons:

- Insufficient management support
- Lack of understanding of the search process
- Focus on reducing cost rather than improving the quality of services

In addition, reliance on PPPs tends to be cyclical. It often coincides with a change in leadership either in HR or top management. Once a program has been adopted or revitalized, it's often implemented throughout the organization, which typically leads to decentralization of the process until the next review or change of leadership returns the focus to corporate headquarters.

Meanwhile, on the consultants' side, PPPs intensify competition both among large search firms and between large and small firms, as more business goes to a smaller number of search firms serving major companies. Search firms become frustrated because it's a big effort to respond, in writing, to numerous detailed questions posed by PPPs that may or may not be relevant to their true capabilities and to make in-person presentations—an especially significant investment of time and expense, given what they see as a slim chance (beyond the natural course of business development) for an important amount of work. And they become cynical because PPPs never work perfectly and sometimes, in fact, have little impact on the flow of assignments to search firms that would have occurred without a PPP.

WHERE WE ARE TODAY

A modern executive recruiting oversight function typically combines the management of internal resources for executive recruiting and hiring with the use of external search and search research services. The leader of the function is often a Director reporting to a VP of Talent Acquisition, a VP of Talent Management, or a Chief Human Resources Officer. Most are one or two steps removed from the CEO and often work with top management on key searches.

At a growing number of companies, the executive recruiting leader participates in internal talent mobility. Most are involved in succession planning, learning to anticipate needs for recruiting externally. The function is aimed at filling positions in the top 1% or 2% of the employee population, although at some companies the role reaches deeper into the organization. If the organization has a global presence, its executive recruiting leader accordingly has a global responsibility, in most cases, although regional HR leaders tend to have influence and sometimes oversight in their markets.

An executive recruiting leader at a large corporation is often responsible for the process of filling about 100 positions per year, with just over half of those being filled with external candidates.

An important trend for large companies is the recruitment of executives directly, rather than through executive search firms (see Chapter 6). Starting with financial institutions, then technology companies, and now companies across industries, in-house search capabilities have grown rapidly in the past 20 years. In the most recent annual ESIX survey of 90 organizations, about half of executives recruited externally came through direct search; about a quarter through search firms; and a smaller fraction through referrals. Most firms now use specialized software to manage client and candidate activity.

Another recent trend has been an expansion of the use of external candidate assessments (beyond what search firms provide). Most companies in the ESIX survey now do this. Most also have a formal onboarding program for newly hired executives.

A key concern for corporate executive recruiting leaders is achieving diversity in the executive population. Few companies are where they want to be and many are devoted to finding better ways to get there (see Chapter 2).

TRAITS OF A GREAT EXECUTIVE RECRUITING INITIATIVE

What does a model executive recruiting initiative look like? An organization that excels in executive recruiting:

- **Gathers information** on all search activity, measures the performance of its search providers, and measures its own behavior in the recruiting process
- **Gives oversight** of search activity to a Director of Executive Recruiting who serves as a center of influence in improving recruiting effectiveness
- **Applies a consistent process** to all search engagements, including a letter of engagement that the hiring organization generates, to set clear expectations about what will happen in the course of the search, and when—and to address issues of fees, expenses, guarantees, cancellations, candidate and client exclusivity, documentation of research, subsequent hires, off-limits protection, responsibilities of the hiring team, and communication patterns during the search
- **Selects search consultants based on performance** and, through the Director, builds long-lasting consulting relationships with search firms that deliver and add value
- **Completes a high percentage of searches**—90% or more of all initiated searches, except for cancellations caused by reorganizations and unforeseen change in business conditions
- **Conducts a thorough process crisply**, with searches averaging 100 to 120 days in length
- On a typical search, **sees an average of four to six candidates** before making an offer
- **Controls the cost of recruiting**, mainly by paying attention to the quality of its process
- As an active partner in the search process, **builds in-house expertise** in identifying and assessing talent—and resources to support that expertise

HOW TO MEASURE EXECUTIVE RECRUITING PERFORMANCE

Improving performance in executive recruiting requires knowing how to measure it and taking the time to do it. We can't afford not to measure the right things, and we can't afford to waste time tracking the wrong things.

Because metrics are more commonly applied to lower-level recruiting, where volume and standardization of process suggest measures such as cost-per-hire, there's a tendency to apply similar measures to executive recruiting. But how useful is a cost-per-hire metric in monitoring search activity that may range from US$200K positions to top-management roles paying millions?

We asked ESIX participants to share their favorite metrics for search activity:

Time-to-fill. Since quality is tougher to measure and cost is less important, this is the most-often-measured feature of the executive search process. Some measure only the overall length of the search, but many break it down to time-to-presentation of candidates and presentation-to-offer acceptance. This provides an opportunity to weigh recruiter performance based on time-to-presentation and -performance of the hiring organization in presentation-to-offer acceptance.

A more advanced way to track time-to-fill is to measure contracted time-to-fill. This takes into account the fact that some searches are urgent, while more time can be devoted to others. So rather than using a standard number of days as a point of reference, the reference can be the number of days assigned to each search as an expectation. The measurement then becomes variance from the expected, or contracted, time to completion.

Cost. *Everyone* measures cost in some form, and specific ways of doing this typically reflect the structure of the executive recruiting function and how search activity is monitored. Obviously, we can tally search fees and related out-of-pocket costs. More interesting is calculating the cost of not hiring—that is, what it costs the organization every month the position is unfilled.

We often hear executive recruiting leaders quote results based on "cost avoidance," whereby they measure the number of searches the in-house team completed, and then calculate what those searches would have cost if they had used a search firm. Thus, the in-house team is measured on what the organization avoided having to spend by not using a search firm.

Quality of service, or in other words, customer satisfaction, using surveys of hiring managers—and often candidates—on how well the executive recruiter performed.

Quality of candidates. Measuring the quality of candidates is the Holy Grail and apparently out of the grasp of most executive recruiting leaders. How can we measure quality of candidates in a way that is practical?

A few companies measure "yield"—the number of candidates interviewed before an offer is made. The lower the average number, the better. Another way, which takes longer, is to measure the performance of hired candidates and track that performance by source of hire. Often, however, that takes too long. Rather than wait a year or two to determine whether this was a high-quality hire, some executive recruiting directors seek an early read (perhaps three months after hiring) on whether the new hire looks like a winner.

Diversity, usually percentages of women and members of underrepresented candidate groups presented and placed.

Search firm performance, typically completion rate, speed, and cost.

Number of searches, number of hires, failed searches, searches in progress, searches on hold.

Direct hires versus external (search firm) hires.
Source of hire.

● ● ●

"Improved quality of hire is by far the most important measure of success. Arguably the only reason to do it is if you can improve the product. Speed and cost, while also important, are weak levers on a relative basis." **– JOHN GOLDBERG, GLOBAL DIRECTOR, EXECUTIVE TALENT ACQUISITION, THE COCA-COLA COMPANY**

IF WE COULD JUST DO THESE THINGS ...

What should a Director of Executive Recruiting be trying to accomplish? We have 11 thoughts about that:

Focus on the *real* business case for managing search activity: higher completion rates, faster searches, higher-quality candidates, and added value (such as market intelligence) from search partnerships and the in-house team.

We made the basic business case above. Beyond those figures, we believe that the logical outcome of better search management includes better candidates as well as a better understanding of the talent market through our search partners or through our own direct recruiting efforts. Remember that leadership recruiting is about solving business problems.

Avoid being driven by reducing search fees. Lower costs will happen as a happy consequence of focusing on the points above, which are much more important to your organization. If you really want the best talent, you probably want the best search consultants (or in-house recruiters) finding it and evaluating it for you, and the best search consultants are in high demand and do not need to discount their fees.

Get top management buy-in. You can't run an effective program without it.

Gather information rigorously on outcomes of all search engagements and use it to inform the search firm selection process.

Don't rush into a preferred-provider program. Spend a year or two managing search activity well. That is, implement a selection and engagement process but hold off on long-term agreements until you have a better written record of search firm performance.

Generate your own engagement letter and use fixed fees. It's your chance to spell out the process as you want it carried out, addressing all the issues that are important to you, setting the schedule of what will happen when, and educating all parties on their roles. Fair (not discounted) fixed fees are cleaner and crisper than percentage fees and should include all expenses except preapproved travel.

Consolidate search activity into partnerships with a short list of large and small firms. Again, this can happen gradually. First you track the activity, then you start steering searches toward the more successful firms. A patient, educated partner in procurement can be a big help here.

Separate the oversight of retained search from contingency recruiting. They're different animals. Retained search is an exclusive (to you) management consulting service. Contingency recruiting is one of many forms of candidate identification—no more, no less.

Establish a sourcing function and combine it with the management of contingency firms. Leverage your efforts to identify potential candidates at the mid-management level.

Down the road, **do some executive recruiting** directly and build your referral program. Once you've got your search management act together, you can consider building an in-house team to handle those searches that make sense (see Chapter 6).

Become a center of influence, not control, on how to use search firms well, and educate the organization on best practices.

Because the hiring manager drives any successful search engagement, that person has to understand all the issues, all the nuances, in working with search firms. These senior people are not always receptive to coaching. This is the most delicate and important role of the Director of Executive Recruiting.

A "TEXTBOOK" EXECUTIVE SEARCH INITIATIVE

At a major financial institution, three things were keeping the SVP of Executive Recruiting and Development awake at night:
- Search firms were being engaged in a variety of informal ways based on relationships and Rolodexes.
- Search firms weren't aligned with any of the bank's internal processes and leadership expectations.
- Internal customers had little access to information on search firm capabilities, success rates, and pricing.

The executive recruiting and development executive led a team of HR professionals, including three managing about 50 external search engagements per year; three conducting about 30 direct searches per year, mostly in HR; and one in "diversity/exploratory recruiting" at the executive level. The bank was spending US$12–US$18 million a year on retained search.

The team took a journey of "easy" steps:

Developing an executive recruiting tool kit

The team reviewed and clarified a seven-step hiring process, from evaluating need to onboarding a hired executive, and mapped it on a supersize page (11x17) for easy reference within what became a complete "User's Guide to Executive Recruiting."

The Guide defined the executive recruiting function and laid out best practices in selecting and engaging a search partner, launching a search, sourcing, interviewing, extending offers, facilitating onboarding, and measuring search firm and candidate performance. Tools included a standard engagement letter, standard terms to use with retained search firms, and a copy of the Client Bill of Rights, Code of Ethics, and Professional Practice Guidelines of the Association of Executive Search and Leadership Consultants (a trade association of leading search firms).

The Guide was then added to the bank's internal HR website as a resource on recruiting to fill positions among the top 1,000 or so of the bank's employees.

Identifying preferred providers

Simultaneously with the first step, the team gathered information on search experiences in all functions and business units, then queried most of the 60 search firms identified. With a goal of selecting a much smaller group of firms to work with more closely, the team narrowed the field, conducted a request for proposals (RFP), cut some more, conducted Q&A with the firms, trimmed the list again against evaluation criteria, and then named about 25 firms to a group of preferred providers. A detailed profile of each firm—its capabilities, performance and internal references—was provided to internal customers online within Executive Recruiting's own website.

Educating internal partners

With a process, providers, and an information resource at hand, the team began an ongoing corporate-wide education initiative by holding a one-day training session for recruiting executives and leadership development partners.

Aligning vendors

Relationship managers from the selected firms spent a half-day at corporate headquarters learning about the bank's expectations, processes, leadership model, and performance tools. Discussions between search consultants and the bank's investor relations team were especially fruitful. The meeting also underlined specific deliverables the team sought in searches for the bank: standardized formats for the job specification, weekly updates, candidate assessments, and reference reports. After the session, HR executives engaged in a meet-and-greet with search consultants in what the HR team felt was a highly productive way to get to know the selected search firms.

Creating a search process consultant role

Key to the success of the program was assigning a member of the executive recruiting team to most searches, to manage the process in collaboration with the hiring manager, HR partner, and executive recruiter.

Keeping score

Partner search firms submitted quarterly reports that were added to internal reports and used to complete each firm's scorecard. Key stats were: number of days up to interview; number of days to close; percent of failed searches (after six months, a search was considered to have failed); diversity of slates; quality of hire (based on performance review one year later); number of searches and fees.

Establishing standard terms

With the exception of a couple of large search firms, selected firms agreed to:

- Tiered pricing, depending on volume and based on cash comp (not sign-ons)
- Payment milestones of one-third on initiation, one-third at 45 days or on presentation of candidates, one-third at start of new hire
- No unspecified expenses or "indirect" fees
- Fee caps
- One-year replacement guarantee, in which the bank had its choice of a fee refund or an expenses-only search
- One-year worldwide off-limits, requiring the search firm to avoid recruiting anyone from the client organization
- A requirement for diverse slates and "value-add services," which typically include market intelligence

The selected large firms agreed to a slightly higher fee scale; payments at initiation, 45 days, and 90 days; negotiated "indirect" fees; and off-limits limited to specified business units and functions.

When selecting search firms, hiring managers then had the benefit of complete information on fees and terms, so they knew what they were spending when they chose. Final search firm selections were made directly from the preferred vendor list, while some searches were awarded after a shootout among two or more firms. And to use a firm not on the preferred vendor list, hiring managers awaited a review of the firm by the executive recruiting team, further encouraging them to use the already-vetted firms.

The overall outcome: a "free market," in which search providers weren't promised engagements but were promoted within the bank based on demonstrated capabilities and performance.

THE BEST-IN-CLASS HEAD OF EXECUTIVE RECRUITING

Dan Barr and Bill Feehan know well the role of head of executive recruiting. Each has been both a head of HR and a search consultant specializing in HR, and so have recruited numerous heads of recruiting, staffing, and talent management to leading companies.

In cooperation with ESIX, Barr and Feehan selected 10 individuals who have served as head of executive recruiting and/or staffing at leading large companies across industries and interviewed them on their professional experiences and knowledge base. The idea was to see what skills and experiences are shared among individuals we consider tops in their field.

Here's what we found: Professionals who advance to this level often have worked in a number of companies and/or or geographies. They have a creative and innovative spirit. They provide "insider" knowledge of the executive search profession and recruiting processes. Over time, they have gained a keen ability to assess talent. Best-in-class performers are sought-after resources who have delivered results. They tend to seek career experiences that will provide them with a broad and strategic perspective.

Experience

A typical best-in-class performer has gained foundational experience in a line of business role such as sales or in a staff role such as finance, communications or human resources. Often, this person will have had early experiences that exposed them to senior management and how to interact with them, including nuances of expressing views in ways that would be respected and acted on.

Best-in-class performers tend to have had experience in recruiting roles early in their careers, as a corporate recruiter or at an executive search or contingency recruiting firm. From there, on the corporate side, some move into a generalist role supporting a line of business, or into a line-of-business role. Ideally, a best-in-class performer has had at least one experience in a line of business or as an integral partner to that business, in order to combine recruiting skills with first-hand understanding of business issues.

Best-in-class performers may move on to corporate recruiting roles with increased responsibilities or continue to advance in an executive search firm. This progression leads to more exposure and interaction with senior executives.

Finally, a best-in-class performer has had exposure to large-volume processes at some point. This might be managing a high-volume recruiting function or working in a specialized staff role related to process management.

Abilities

- Best-in-class performers are recognized authorities on talent and talent acquisition. They have a passion for recruiting, a deep understanding of the business and organization culture, and highly developed sales skills. This translates into credibility with internal clients, external search partners and candidates.

• They have a strong executive presence that enables them to influence and facilitate the hiring of executive talent.

• They possess exceptional relationship management, assessment, and coaching skills.

• They know their business, its strategy, culture, and leadership requirements and have a keen understanding of the organization's value proposition, with the ability to convey it compellingly to candidates.

• They understand general business trends and issues both within and outside their industry and geographic focus.

• They are experts in executive search and each step in the search process. They know how to select search firms; negotiate fees, terms and conditions; and monitor effectiveness.

• They have mastered executive compensation and how to develop competitive packages.

• They have a sales orientation, know sales techniques and how to close deals.

• At the same time, they need to have a process orientation and an interest in metrics, tracking, trends, analysis and reporting. That's all it takes!

THE YIN AND YANG OF EXECUTIVE SEARCH

There is a dualism in the executive search process that, when successful, accommodates contrasting characteristics in what we might think of as a delicate balance.

Hard skills	and	Soft skills
Manage	and	Lead
Experience	and	Relationship
Transact	and	Consult
Assess	and	Recruit
Contingency	and	Retainer
Commodity	and	Service
Specialist	and	Generalist
Speed	and	Momentum
Cost	and	Value
Results	and	Quality

2.

THE SEARCH PROCESS
• • •

MAKING THE DECISION TO GO OUTSIDE

A search is launched when it's become clear that no internal candidate is the right person, or that there's a desire to compare an internal candidate with externals who might be recruited.

This decision may be clear from the start, but unfortunately some searches are launched before the hiring organization is certain of its mission. This is a recipe for failure and the organization will likely end up in a place it didn't want to be. To quote the Cheshire Cat, speaking to Alice in *Alice in Wonderland*, if you're not sure where you're going, "then it doesn't much matter which way you go."

It's a good time to ask ourselves: How integrated is our executive recruiting function with our organization's succession planning function?

Many companies are in the position of trying to strengthen this relationship. It begins with having an organized way of making the decision to go outside at the executive level. Experience indicates that decisions to recruit or promote are typically made as much on instinct as on available information on who may be capable.

Perhaps, each time we make this choice, we should look at the pros and cons:

Why go outside?	Why promote?
• No internal candidate ready	• Qualified or developable internal candidate
• General talent need in function	• Avoid alienating team members
• New line of business	• Not enough time to search outside
• Market intelligence	• More flexibility in assigning internals
• Diversity	• Know internals' strengths better
• New skills/culture	• Unwilling to pay premium for outsider
• Confidence in search process	• Search fees, or in-house team costs
• Confidence in hiring process	• Higher risk of outside exec leaving
• Marquee player may bring other	• Low confidence in search process
• If international, local know-how	• Low confidence in hiring process

Many feel that there's an inherent advantage in developing talent rather than recruiting it, but these lists indicate as many possible reasons for going outside as for promoting from within. Use them as a checklist: Which apply to the case at hand?

We tossed this around at an ESIX roundtable discussion and got the following comments:

• "We go outside because it's a lot easier than grappling with internal politics."

• "We're developing better information on internal candidates, to give them the edge."

• "We find it very difficult to go outside in general, so we encourage our hiring executives to look harder internally."

• "We often have a search firm compare internal versus external candidates, based on our corporate competencies."

• "We find a lot of resistance to going outside. Insiders have a faster learning curve."

- "Some jobs always go outside—business development, deal-makers. But in startup mode, sometimes you can start with an internal person, then decide whether to go outside. "

THE EXECUTIVE SEARCH PROCESS CHECKLIST

Clarify the Need and Develop a Strategy
_____ Identify and validate the need. Is it clear? Are there internal candidates?

_____ Establish hiring team and brief them on the process.

_____ Develop initial position spec:
> Primary responsibilities and reporting relationships
> How the role may evolve

_____ Develop initial compensation target.

_____ Search directly or use a search firm?

_____ Any issues of confidentiality?

_____ Local candidates or relocation?

Select a Search Partner (if you are using one)
_____ Identify external search consultants with relevant track records.

_____ Solicit information to document capabilities.

_____ Check references.

_____ Meet with the two or three most qualified consultants.

_____ Discuss where and how candidates will be identified.

_____ Discuss potential conflicts and obstacles.

_____ Seek fee bids and acceptance of engagement terms.

_____ Establish time frame for each step in the search.

Begin the Search
_____ Meet with external search consultant or in-house recruiter to discuss the role in depth.

_____ Collectively agree on the job specification.

_____ Identify known potential candidates and referral sources.

_____ Schedule likely candidate interview dates for hiring team.

Calibrate Candidates
_____ Meet with recruiter to discuss long list.

_____ Review implications: Adjust job spec? Access new candidate pools?

_____ Conduct weekly phone updates on candidate development.

Interview Candidates
_____ Full briefing for hiring team before each candidate interview.
_____ Structured interviews with immediate, detailed feedback.
_____ Identify and pursue two finalists.
_____ Second interviews, further assessment.
_____ Additional reference checking and background verification.

Extend an Offer
_____ Develop the offer and preview it to the selected candidate.
_____ Extend the offer.

Facilitate Onboarding
_____ Develop onboarding plan.
_____ Process new-hire paperwork.
_____ Hand off to leadership development group.
_____ Follow up regularly.

HOW TO MANAGE A SEARCH ENGAGEMENT

Let's take a closer look at how the search process plays out. It is fraught with potential for delays, lost opportunities, and ultimately, failure to achieve objectives. Detours can be traced back to unrealistic or misplaced expectations and second-guessing in what is admittedly a subjective undertaking.

An executive search is a dynamic process in which simultaneous activities are coordinated by frequent, concise exchanges of information. Fundamentally, it's shared by the hiring executive and the executive recruiter (in-house recruiter and/or external search consultant) in a partnership requiring full cooperation and communication. Together, they can avoid costly pitfalls and safeguard success by being decisive and accountable.

The initial draft of the job specification ("spec") is key. It will include specific responsibilities of the position, reporting relationships, required experience, desired educational background, personal characteristics, and likely places where such candidates may be found. Creating the job spec offers an important opportunity to outline specific outcomes the organization seeks from this position in the next year or two. This outline can be used later to measure the performance of the hired candidate and how well the organization has supported its goals.

Next, the hiring decision process must be made clear. Who will participate in interviews? Everyone involved must understand that the decision to hire will rest only with the hiring executive, with the concurrence of their superior.

What compensation will be required to attract excellent candidates to the position? Start with the best information at hand and continue to refine this expectation during candidate research and development.

Is this a confidential search? If so, executive search firms are well equipped to conduct a search without identifying the hiring organization, although this can introduce limitations on candidate development. There are options for in-house teams to conduct similar searches, though more on an exploratory basis.

What is the scope of the search? Local, regional, national, global? This has implications for the resources needed to execute the search.

When these issues have been addressed by the hiring team, the in-house recruiter and hiring executive select a search methodology (either in-house or external search firm; see Chapter 3). At the same time, the recruiter responsible for the search drafts a position specification aimed at selling the opportunity to top prospective candidates. The position specification is based on the internal initial job spec but would not include information about the search strategy. It would include an overview of the organization and salient points about why someone would be attracted to the role.

The search begins officially when the hiring team—hiring executive, in-house recruiter, and possibly external search consultant—adopt an agreed version of the position spec and achieve a full understanding of where the recruiter will look, how the recruiter will look, how they will report progress, and how the course will be corrected if necessary. This should be confirmed in writing.

The in-house recruiter and hiring executive should check two things carefully here: Does the recruiter have a full understanding of the organization's strategy and culture as well as the details of the position being filled? Also, have all members of the hiring team pledged not to undermine or circumvent the recruiter in identifying and recommending candidates? All candidates should be evaluated through the same comprehensive process.

About four weeks into the search—or sooner, if the team has put the search on a fast track—the recruiter should deliver a progress report. Ideally, this report includes:

- A summary of findings about the market and potential

candidates, including comments on the general qualifications and interest of candidates contacted; a reading on whether the compensation target will hold; and any useful information about how the client is viewed

• A complete list of sources and potential candidates contacted, and the outcome

• A brief written summary for each candidate developed sufficiently to indicate further discussion, followed by the candidate's resume

The hiring team then promptly conducts a review to determine whether research is delivering desired results, where else to look, and whether any changes in the spec are necessary.

Within six weeks after launch, the recruiter should begin presenting candidates. During this stage, hiring team members must put top priority on being available and prepared for interviews. All of them must be conscious of their responsibility to sell the organization and opportunity. Interviewers should receive background materials well in advance of each interview. They should make detailed notes immediately after the interview. And the recruiter should debrief interviewers and candidates within 24 hours.

No more than three or four final candidates are asked to participate in a second interview.

How to close a search

Momentum is critical to a successful conclusion, and the in-house recruiter is responsible for maintaining it, with the support of the hiring executive. Speed and decisiveness capture and maintain momentum, which is vital to keeping the best candidates interested and giving the hiring team the confidence to move toward an offer. The selling process must continue. The interviewing team must be fully engaged. Emotion will peak in this process and the hiring team must be prepared to act when it does.

When a second interview is scheduled, reference-checking should begin. In addition to anecdotal comments from references, the process should include verifying the candidate's education credentials, dates of employment, and compensation expectations. Also, court, motor vehicle, and credit records should be checked.

Once the leading candidate has been identified, the recruiter determines what needs to be included in the offer, and what the make-

or-break issues are. An offer is then developed with the hiring executive. The goal here is to make the first offer the one that will be accepted, and it's the recruiter's responsibility that this occurs. (However, the recruiter also develops an offer for a backup candidate should the lead candidate turn down their offer.) The offer letter should come immediately after the offer-triggering interview. A reasonable period should be given for a response (one intervening weekend).

Candidates who are not selected should be turned off very nicely by the recruiter, by telephone (not by leaving a message).

Where to leave the map

When there's a choice, common sense must always take precedence over procedure. The recruiting team must be able to recognize, in the no-two-searches-alike world of executive recruiting, that some situations that call for a departure from process. Knowing when to break policy is just as important as knowing when to follow it.

Perhaps the key place to leave the map is the point at which it becomes apparent that the search isn't working.

"A lot of our searches don't go well, so I spend my life redirecting searches," reports Meg Staunton, VP Executive Recruiting, XPO Logistics. "We consider organization design and how else we might structure a team in order to get the talent we need. I also like to think out of the box, looking at super-smart people in different industries who may not look like their experience is on target, but who can do the job."

Creating opportunities

It's also possible to leave the map for positive reasons—even before a proper search is in progress. Here's an anecdote from Adriana Quevedo, Executive Recruiting Director at Intel:

> *A few years ago, I participated in a Women in Leadership conference for $49. (Yes, it was only $49!)*
>
> *My expectations were low, especially because the event wasn't oriented to the high-tech industry, but there was a panel discussion that captured my attention. The panel was composed of five very talented women in leadership positions in various industries. Two stood out, and I introduced myself and brought back their business cards and bios. My Executive Recruiter reached out to one who seemed she could be a good fit for Intel. We suggested her to two business units. Both liked her and one moved quickly toward*

making her an offer.

Imagine—she wasn't looking for a job, we had no open position for her, and even if we could create one, it would not carry the VP title she already had. What we could offer was flexibility in her schedule. That became an attraction point.

We made the hire. She became extremely successful and now carries the VP title as well as a flexible schedule."

GETTING THE MOST FROM YOUR SOURCES

Arguably the most important part of the search process comes early, in the sourcing step.

Search consultant Sharon Rubin Stein has mastered the art of the telephone interview and taught many search practitioners how to maximize the return on investment in initial contact with sources and potential candidates. She offers the following advice:

To identify sources and potential candidates, a search consultant uses professional contacts, referrals, original research, the consultant's own database, conference attendee lists, networking, thought leaders in the relevant industry and function, editors at trade magazines, conference speakers who can provide referrals ... the list is never complete.

Initial calls are more effective when they are not cold calls. Get referrals. The best source is the person who just left the organization you're targeting. If you don't have appropriate contacts in your network, you can easily find these folks on LinkedIn.

The first referral suggestions you'll receive will be people who are looking for their next role, who may not be the most desirable prospective candidates. Everyone likes to help out a buddy. But when enticed to open up, sources can offer much more.

Pre-references can be done on nearly every potential candidate before you launch a call to them. In this way, you make smart calls to A players.

When sources resist having you use their name with a potential candidate, see what the reason is. You can also offer to use the source's name in this way: "Chris Smith doesn't think you are looking for your next opportunity but said you might be knowledgeable in this arena and well-connected. I'm hoping to get the benefit of your thoughts on this assignment."

Where do you start on a call/pitch? Begin by painting a broad picture of the client organization, its mission and vision. Then funnel down to more specificity. Establish credibility and rapport. Who do we know in common? Use flattery: "Jane says you're terrific!"

Humor is your best ally. If the call is enjoyable, the source will share more. Don't be afraid to digress from your task or seem less goal-oriented.

When the prospect/source picks up your call, after you introduce yourself, ask, "Do you have time to talk?" If they have only five minutes, resist the temptation to pitch, assess, or source them. Give the reason for your call, say it's a very important search. Ask, "Can we schedule a time to talk?" Sometimes they immediately say they do have some time, and most are willing to schedule a call.

Send spec before screening? Some do, but some wait until the candidate shows more interest and/or is clearly well-qualified. It can be better to limit the sending of the spec to avoid a barrage of inquiries from candidates who are not qualified. In addition, if you send a spec, you lose the advantage of being able to provide color or context around the role. Often, candidates or sources will misconstrue even the most well-written spec (or may think they aren't perfectly qualified) and they self-select out. It's important to create a dialogue.

In giving a pitch, use compelling facts about the organization and role. Use success stories (e.g., the role is open due to promotion).

While presenting the role, what do we listen for? Are candidates asking questions? Making appreciative sounds? Write down what they are attracted to. This info can be used later when trying to close the candidate to a meeting.

Decide if this is a candidate or a source. Screen out, not in. Keep a list of qualifiers. Does the candidate match up? When you find one big non-starter, change course and make it a source call.

To save time while assessing a candidate, use fact-based, closed-ended questions addressing all the qualifiers. If the candidate meets all of your criteria and is "still standing," finish the call with a specific, clear next step.

Meanwhile, see how much you can learn: How big is your team? How is it structured? To whom do you report? How many steps from the top? Who reports to you? (Number, titles, functions, indirects) Corporate or shared service model? Peers in the business units? Matrixed? Where do peers report? Who is the key client you support? And you're one of how many people who reports to your boss? How is your job different from those in business units? How long have you been in the role? (If new, this person is a source for their former organization.) Not only will these questions help determine the fit of this particular individual, but you'll also know where else in the organization other suitable candidates might be found (e.g., in corporate versus a business unit).

If the person meets all qualifications, let the sales process begin.

How do you get them to invest in the process? Now ask open-ended questions. Get them to talk about themselves. Make them the expert. Meanwhile, start looking for holes where you can make life better for them. In doing so, be careful with reinforcement of where they are now, or they will start selling you on why they shouldn't move.

What else to do on this call? Ask questions designed to get yes answers—get them used to saying "yes." Would you like to run a P&L? Bigger P&L? Is managing people one of your key strengths?

If the prospective candidate indicates they are not interested, "No" is where the sale begins. Present more compelling facts. Use humor, ask more questions. The best candidates will almost always say no at first.

The final question before close: "Does this intrigue you enough to talk further?" It's more likely to get a yes than "Can we meet?" as there's very little commitment involved.

If there's resistance, take the pressure off. "Would you like to know what the process is like?" Stein tells the potential candidate it will take time, "so they feel it's safe to get into the water."

High achievers may resist or even fear change. First make an appreciative comment such as, "I understand why you might feel that way." Make them feel heard. Then provide more compelling facts about the client organization/role: "Here's why you might be a success." Or have them come in to meet one person. Less pressure. Just a conversation.

But if the person is not a candidate: "Perhaps you would not be well served in this role." Give to get. "What kind of role do you think would be ideal for you?" "Are you open to relocation?" etc. Let them know you will keep them in mind for future opportunities.

Now turn them into a source. Best order of sourcing questions: Do you have a recommendation for me? Who are your competitors? Who do you know there? Is there anyone from your last organization whom I should talk to?

Dig and map the entire last organization: "Do you belong to any relevant organizations? Do they have conferences? Would you please send me the attendee list?" "Who's blocked from promotion at your current organization?" "Who's the best at your current firm?" (last question, least likely to answer).

Then: Always ask if you can use their name.

Back to the initial call that yields a strong candidate not yet showing interest: When is no really no? It's really no when the candidate is divorced with children in the city, or has just relocated, has ailing parents or high school–age children, if the in-laws live across the street, if the house is $500K under water, or if the candidate is simply making too much money.

By the way—if when you pitch, you get a "yes" immediately, be suspicious and check "back-door" references.

How many times do you call a perfect candidate? Until they take the call.

Sharon Rubin Stein is a Managing Director at ZRG Partners in New York.

SUCCESS FACTORS IN EXECUTIVE RECRUITING

Directors of Executive Recruiting have many a story about searches gone wrong. The Executive Search Information Exchange engaged in a root-cause analysis exercise, sometimes called the "Five Whys" because it consists of asking why something happened, followed by more "whys" until a root cause is established.

The exercise delivered a long list of root causes for failed searches. We then determined the opposite of each root cause of failure in order to create a list of factors that presumably would lead to success. For example, we found that lack of top management support for the search process was in some cases a root cause for a failed search. So, we concluded that top management support for the process can be a success factor.

Here are success factors in executive recruiting:

Top management support
- Process and engagement are based in a well-developed corporate initiative
- CEO actively supports a consistent process even at highest levels

It's key that the organization's leadership actively supports of this type of initiative, perhaps more so than other programs due to the sensitivity of the work and the senior level of leadership involved. A better word might be "sponsorship" rather than "support," as such a program will take some time to deliver tangible results, and even longer to make the high-value strategic impact that is possible.

Solid succession planning
- We know why we're going outside
- No "pop-up" internal candidates
- There's time to conduct the search well

An in-house executive recruiting function should work in partnership with an internal talent management function. In fact, in some organizations, these two functions both report to the same leader, which makes a lot of sense. Either way, they need to communicate on a regular and frequent basis, so that a complete map of the internal and external talent landscape can be created.

It will then be clear when and why we might make the decision to go externally for leadership talent, and—as we will discuss in Chapter 6—can create long-term talent pipelines with clarity and intensity. This will also give us the proper time needed to complete each search, even if it's in reaction to a short-term need.

Furthermore, with a complete picture of the internal and external talent, it is less likely that an internal candidate will pop up unexpectedly after the first four or five external candidate interviews. This happens all too often: Once the interview team starts to get a picture of the type of candidate they are looking for, they start to remember colleagues from other internal groups who might be good for the role.

At that point, the recruiting team has spoken to a significant number of external candidates and brought some in for interviews. If we then tell the external market that we are canceling the search after only a few weeks, it leaves a bad impression on what is likely to be a small talent pool and muddies the water for future searches. Further, at this point, the search has racked up notable costs in search fees or internal resources, and often both. Establishing up front that no "pop-up" internal candidates will be allowed avoids these pitfalls.

Real and well-defined need
- Purpose of the search is clear
- Reporting relationships are clear
- Compensation expectations are realistic
- Location and job features are established

- Criteria for "fit" are quantified
- There is consensus on the above points and on this: the hiring executive, superiors, and peers understand and agree with the specific need

Having full clarity and consensus on what type of leader the business needs is critical. One of the most important roles of a true trusted-advisor recruiter is to get to this point of clarity. Not only is this important for executing the search at hand and making sure the interview team are all on the same page, but it is critical for the long-term success of the candidate.

Through our consulting we need to ask: Why do we need this role? Who will this person report to and liaise with on a regular basis? How will we compensate them? and What goals will we focus their motivation and rewards on?

These are all questions that will help us execute the search and persuade the best talent to consider moving from their current success path.

Right search consultant is engaged
- Knows the client's organization
- Has highly relevant recent experience
- Has performed well in the past (check references); is credible
- Has capacity to make the search a priority
- Can access potential candidates (e.g., who is off limits?)
- Will represent the organization well
- Is client-service driven
- Can add value beyond filling the position

The right recruiter could be an in-house consultant as well as an external search firm recruiter. Ideally, the consultant will know the client's organization, though at the same time be confident and consultative enough to be able to push back for the greater good of the organization, rather than just wishing to please the hiring manager. The consultant should have highly relevant, recent experience, and should have performed well in the past. If they are external, then it is important for the hiring group to contact other clients for references.

For both in-house and external consultants: Do they have the capacity to make the search a priority? The function's credibility rests on each search it executes, so each should be seen as a priority. For an external recruiter: Can all potential candidates be approached, or are there off-limits agreements we should know about? How many of these off-limits agreements apply, and with which organizations? If only a few, then perhaps an in-house recruiter can approach the candidates.

Often missed, but as important when evaluating external recruiters, is to ask what value the recruiter can add beyond just filling the position. Are they able to provide market intelligence on the talent, the compensation being offered, or perhaps on the hiring group's reputation in the market? Could they help persuade the hiring manager to go in the direction favored by the larger organization?

It must be said that a consultant's words, even when the same as an in-house recruiter's, can have the halo effect of an outsider's confirming view.

Everyone understands their roles

- Hiring executive drives process and owns the final hiring decision
- Executive recruiter (in-house or external) advises/executes process
- HR/recruiting executive facilitates process
- Everyone makes the search a priority (available and prepared for interviews)
- Everyone has a role in selling the opportunity and moving toward closure

Some hiring managers seem to believe that recruiting is the sole responsibility of the recruiting team. This is a bit like saying the goalie on a hockey team is the only person responsible for making sure the other team doesn't score.

Not true. Everyone has a role to play, from beginning to end. But this should be clear: The hiring manager owns the hiring decision and cannot be absolved if the hire goes wrong!

The in-house recruiter owns the process, advising the client and executing various aspects of the hiring mechanism. Sometimes a human resources business partner is involved, and they can be very helpful in assisting in the process, perhaps persuading the hiring manger to keep to long-term organization goals, as opposed to short-term wins. They can also provide context on group dynamics and culture.

It's key to ensure that everyone makes the role a priority for as long as the search lasts, and it should also be made clear that everyone has a role in selling the opportunity to the finalist candidate.

Expectations are clear
- Job description is specific and complete
- Compensation range is set—but realistically flexible
- Time frame is understood; a good search takes at least 12 weeks
- Momentum—not speed per se—is key
- Calibration of candidates, adjustments, and flexibility are needed

We have various tools to ensure that everyone is on the same page, whether it's their role in the process as outlined above, or whether there's clarity on the need—but probably the most important is the job description.

Having said that, even though we can work toward perfect clarity, we are not buying boxes at a fixed price with specific dimensions. We're working with a fluid marketplace influenced by many uncertain factors, and we are "buying" talent, both of which have a host of various dimensions, some of which we can see and some of which we might not see for some time.

Therefore, we will also have to be flexible on compensation ranges, for example, and timing of the search. As we reach out to more prospects in the market, the information we glean will help to adjust the requirement for the role as well as perhaps the compensation range, and we will need to be ready for such changes.

Rigorous research
- Beyond LinkedIn, and beyond screening the obvious
- Exhaustive sourcing to identify A-plus players
- Special efforts to find diverse prospects (include in contract terms?)

Although various software programs and social media platforms have helped shed more light on the talent market, they are never the one-stop shop, and either our in-house teams or our external consultants need to be constantly scouring the talent market in creative ways. Further, we need to go above and beyond finding the "usual suspects" and ensure that we're bringing diverse talent to the table.

Insightful, persuasive candidate development
- Recruiter skills that generate interest among those most

difficult to attract
- A willingness to ignore assumptions and pursue out-of-box possibilities
- Assessment for potential and "culture add"
- Candidate write-ups that address the match with criteria and company expectations

This is where great recruiters really shine. They are fearless and determined to reach prospects whom others would give up on. They ignore assumptions on whether someone will even take a call and pursue creative possibilities that expand the potential talent pool. Some say the very best recruiters are so persistent they will not stop trying to reach a prospect until they have at least heard a firm "not interested"—if not a cease-and-desist order.

Once a prospect becomes a candidate, a brief is written to explain their candidacy. It should include the key job criteria and how the candidate fares against them, as well as candidate motivations, willingness to relocate if necessary, compensation expectations, and ideally some level of background referencing. Education and career verification can come later (though a search firm should provide it early on).

"Just because senior executives know how to run a company or a division, it does not mean they also know best practices for running an interview process. They need guidance and counsel." —**SCOTT LONG, DIRECTOR, GLOBAL EXECUTIVE SEARCH, TERADATA**

Solid interview process
- Structured interviews; a total of five is plenty
- Avoidance of the "Spanish Inquisition" team interview
- Only two rounds of 1:1 interviews of 45 to 60 minutes each
- Immediate feedback; the number-one shortfall of hiring organizations is failing to provide detailed interview feedback on each candidate

We are told that structured behavioral interviews are one of the most trusted and consistent ways of assessing candidates, and naturally, a consistent and well-managed interview process is best for everyone concerned. Our research and experience tell us that around five or six interviews are probably best for each candidate, though there are different interview models out there. Some organizations, particularly research-oriented ones, prefer to use a panel method, while others have the candidate present a speech to a group of peers as part of the assessment process; these methods, however, are both in the minority.

In most cases, there are a number of one-on-one interviews, typically lasting around an hour and occurring over one or two days. The second interview day is often combined with area and property tours if relocation is involved, and might include a family visit.

Interview feedback appears to be a consistent problem across regions and industries, particularly at the senior leadership level, and we cover this is more depth in Chapter 5.

Effective communication

- Regular, clear, concise updates
- What's new this week?
- Where does each candidate stand?
- What are we learning in the market?
- How is this affecting our expectations and our search plan?
- And later in the process: Who is checking references? Who is checking background/social?

Communication is a part of the job search that needs to be highlighted in its own right. None of the success factors discussed above can be achieved without continuous, clear, and effective communication. It's critical that the recruiting team, including the hiring manager, holds regular update meetings, ideally at least every two weeks if not weekly. These are not only to discuss process updates and new candidates, but also to share market information and feedback that frontline recruiters may be hearing from the general talent pool. This information, especially candidate compensation expectations, will likely help to steer the search plan and reduce surprises later in the process.

Relatively early on, the process of referencing should be discussed to determine what references should be checked and how, and who is responsible for which part. We have heard of instances where less experienced hiring managers have taken it upon themselves to do "back-door" references on candidates and even early prospects, which can put the candidate's career at risk with their current organization and exposes the hiring organization to possible legal liabilities.

It is also important that all parties keep each other informed of changes in the internal business environment as organizations and business strategies—and therefore talent needs—change.

Great candidate experience

- It's a marketing issue; each candidate is a customer, a prospect
- We're recruiting, not screening
- Strong candidates have options and other offers
- Relationships are a two-way street
- If relocation is indicated, engage the family early and often; roll out the red carpet and let kids come along
- Close the loop; lack of closure is the top complaint of candidates, and candidates talk

These days it hardly needs to be said that recruiting is as much a marketing/sales function as it is about hiring. Each prospect or candidate is likely a customer or an influencer, so it's simply good business to treat candidates well. Many organizations have perfected a white-glove experience for senior candidates, going the extra mile with private car service, tickets to local events and gifts in hotel rooms.

At the senior level, we are mostly recruiting candidates rather than screening them out. Strong talent has options and often other offers, and in most cases is currently well-paid in a senior role. While the power to decide who and when to hire once belonged entirely to the organization, in today's environment, top candidates have greater control over where to take their career.

We suggest discovering the decision influencers: the spouse, and sometimes children and extended family, especially if relocation is required. They should be engaged early, even if only indirectly. In the case of relocation, when the time comes for touring the new location, it should be a red-carpet experience for those influencers. A few hundred dollars for extra flights and hotel rooms might make the difference in a million-dollar hire! Remember, we're not just selling furniture. We change lives—and not just our hire's. Our decisions impact spouses and their careers, children and their schools and friends, perhaps aging parents, and the communities they are engaged in.

Each of these possible impacts should be explored as soon as possible, within reason and legal/ethical limits.

Do not overlook rejected candidates in your approach to the candidate experience, especially silver medalists. They may have a future with your organization down the line—and even if not, you want to leave people with a favorable impression of your hiring process.

Crisp decision-making

- Compensation partner is engaged throughout
- Speedy development of offers
- Any movement in hiring strategy is communicated immediately to recruiter
- Offers are made quickly
- Offers are never rejected (recruiter's responsibility)

As an extension of candidate experience, and likely as a response to a highly competitive talent market, making talent decisions quickly is key. Not only is there a chance that we might lose our favorite candidate if we do not do this, but we are also not showing respect to those senior executives who spent their valuable time interviewing with us, and some of whom also inconvenienced their families to do the same.

To hasten a speedy offer, some organizations pre-negotiate special compensation package ranges with their executive compensation partners and, if necessary, with their board of directors. This happens especially in hypercompetitive markets where special stock awards might be necessary to close finalist candidates, and every second counts when the competition is doing the same thing.

Successful close

- Hiring manger fully engaged; senior leaders can assist
- Regular contact with candidates
- Motivation and hot-button issues identified
- Coaching on candidate's exit from current role and preparation for counteroffer

The closing process is a particularly stressful time, yet also the most exciting part of the recruitment process, and it's a critical time for the interviewing team to engage. We call this the "hearts and minds" process, where interviewers who particularly clicked with the candidate are asked to connect with them in a carefully structured approach.

For instance, after an offer has been made, the hiring manager is asked to email the candidate immediately in a "soft" way (i.e., with limited pressure) to suggest that the candidate should feel comfortable contacting them as they think through the offer. In the next day or so, one of these interviewers can then message the candidate, saying they're excited to hear they might be working together soon. A couple of days later, another interviewer can send a reference to a topic that was discussed in their interview.

Perhaps a day or two after that, the hiring manager can call the candidate at home—perhaps even catch the spouse—and offer to provide any further information that may be needed.

Throughout this process, the recruiter is constantly in contact with the candidate too, gauging feelings and trying to understand what the "influencers" (family, etc.) are saying behind the scenes. In the same time frame, a tailored gift would go to the candidate, sent in a way to make sure the family also sees the goodies, if possible.

Throughout the closing process, the recruiter should be working to understand the candidate's hot buttons and motivations in general, and perhaps tweaking offer details to facilitate these needs.

Crucially at this time, the recruiter should be "pre-closing"—in other words, testing the waters with the candidate before anything comes out in writing, to make sure that when the final offer comes along, it's almost exactly what the candidate was expecting and possibly including an added sweetener.

The growing likelihood that candidates will receive a counteroffer from their current employer should be addressed early on, and the candidate should be coached on what might happen—especially if you know the pattern that the competition usually follows, and in what ways emotions and compensation are often used. It's important to remind the candidate why they are talking to you in the first place, what it is that they told you early on was their motivation for looking outside their current organization, and how a sudden show of love from their current employer might not last long if the candidate chooses to stay. At this point, you might add that there is some evidence that a high percentage of candidates who accept counteroffers leave their organization with a year.

"Cover the counter-offer over and over," advises Jeff Boag, Global Director of Executive Recruiting at Melaleuca. "The market is too competitive and top performers are gold, so make sure candidates are well prepared for the counter-offer."

Effective onboarding
- The most valuable part of the hiring process

- Includes development opportunities identified during the search
- Not difficult, though too often neglected

ONBOARDING PROGRAM LENGTH

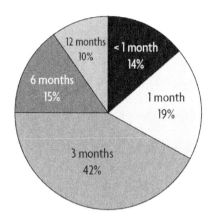

We have often stated that onboarding is perhaps the most valuable part of the hiring process—and yet too often, it's neglected. We have recently seen an uptick in interest in executive onboarding through our Annual Benchmark Survey, however, which is an excellent move in the right direction: In our 2019 survey of 107 organizations, 66% of respondents have formal executive-level onboarding programs of some kind, which is up from 54% in the previous year. Most of these have a three-month tenure.

It is generally a best practice for these onboarding programs to include development information gleaned through both the interview and assessment process, as well as that ascertained through references.

TACTICS AND TOOLS TO IMPROVE DIVERSITY HIRING

In recent years, with diversity hiring such a high priority, the following themes come up consistently in our webinars and roundtable discussions:

- The overall plan should be holistic, including the recruiting team, the talent management function, employee resource groups, and outside partners such as executive search firms.
- Senior leadership should not only sponsor and support the

efforts but be actively involved as part of the recruiting team.
• Activities and results should be tracked and reported, ideally publicly; transparency is key, even if painful.
• Target talent should include midlevel as well as senior executives—a "buy-to-build" approach.
• Focus on creating long-term diverse leadership pipelines and communities for external talent.
• Diverse interviewers on candidate loops are a basic requirement, keeping in mind that it can be taxing on the internal diverse population.

● ● ●

"Putting in place a mandate for diverse slates (candidates and interview panels) is a lot more difficult than you might expect."
—TINA WITZKE, SENIOR DIRECTOR, EXECUTIVE TALENT ACQUISITION, ADP

In a webinar on the subject, including a panel of leaders from Facebook, Google, Intel, and Microsoft, we learned that most use the following tactics:
• Unconscious-bias training for all leaders
• Leaders' diversity goals tied to their bonuses
• Quotas for diverse slating, though this is also a point of contention
• Hiring-manager coaching to help leaders think pragmatically about requirements
• Focused job descriptions, away from vagaries and toward specific skills

And in a further follow-up ESIX study, we find that the definition of diversity is evolving from a few underrepresented groups into the realm of "diversity of thought," with much more talk about inclusion and belonging. In fact, one definition of diversity encompasses "physical, societal, occupational, relational, and mental differences." A quote from diversity and inclusion strategist Vernā Myers further illuminates this: "Diversity is being invited to the party, inclusion is actually being asked to dance."[®]

Recent research also reveals a more positive tone regarding wins and achievements. It seems that the last few years of constant focus on hiring diverse leaders, along with a gain in visibility and attention to diversity brought by external factors in many countries and industries, is making an impact in a number of organizations.

A Success Story in Recruiting for Diversity

Rebecca Foden, Head of Talent Acquisition & Diversity at Transport for London, shares this story of how her team expanded its overall effectiveness through recruiting for diversity:

> *To address diversity at the executive level, we adopted a model we call "Core, Close, Creative," and were able to hire more than 50% diverse leadership talent (women and ethnic minorities). The model challenges perceptions that skills have a shelf life of three to five years.*
>
> *It starts with Core, which are the traditional target organizations, then makes a push to find hidden talent from transferable (Close) industries, and then to Creative, where we look in completely different industries. The businesses are completely engaged in this process, as we need fresh thinking, and diversity of thought enables a more diverse organization.*
>
> *Next the team turned to internal talent, curious about the idea of a forgotten middle, and possibly a diverse talent pool. Wider engagement and greater collaboration with employee resource groups has created a groundswell movement of internal talent to take greater career risk, to lean in and apply for roles.*
>
> *Emboldened by this, our team delivered leadership spotlight events and internal career events to highlight opportunities and showcase roles in cross-functional areas. It's a brave and innovative team with a very small budget but which has moved from a transactional role to a strategic one by taking a scientific approach, advising senior leaders, and using talent intelligence and creative flair to help make the impossible possible.*

Executive Introductions, with Diversity as a Bonus

An initiative at Comcast has delivered unexpected benefits in recruiting for diversity. Beth Bunting, VP of Executive Search and Talent Management, explains:

> *Several years ago, we built our Executive Introduction framework. We realized that, in the moment of the transaction, when a hiring leader is anxious about having a gap in their leadership structure, it's difficult for them to expand their thinking about what success might look like beyond the "Qualifications"*

bullet of the job description.

With Executive Introduction, we proactively introduce talent to the leaders "between requisitions" as a way to get them thinking about new options. Though this is not designed as a diversity program, our hires through EI are currently 45% people of color and 55% women—proving that the proactive efforts have incredible impact.

ON COMPENSATION TRANSPARENCY

Recently passed laws on pay in the US, aimed at reducing gender bias, have curtailed the once-common practice of asking candidates about their compensation history. How are companies addressing this?

A quick survey of 74 leading companies finds that nearly 80% quickly removed references to compensation in their application process, that 75% conduct in-house training for their employees and 50% created US-wide policies in response to the new laws.

The basic difference is that instead of asking candidates about their compensation history, companies are asking candidates about their compensation expectations. However, if a candidate volunteers information about compensation history, that's fair game (though it might be illegal to record the data).

FOR A COMPELLING OFFER, CASH IS TOP TACTIC

Many factors outside of compensation contribute to developing an offer that will bring a desired candidate over the finish line. But as far as compensation goes, cash bonuses are used most often to win acceptance.

ESIX surveyed 80 leading organizations across industries, globally, and found that two-thirds use cash bonuses in some form to supplement offers at the executive level—far ahead of any other single tactic. These cash bonus offers are used not to attract candidates, but to offset losses a finalist candidate might experience in accepting the new role. Such a bonus is generally based on estimated losses in the upcoming 12 months of earnings, though this varies in some cases, and is not always at 100% replacement value.

Meanwhile, some companies use equity to replace potential losses and among those. Again, most are attempting to address the upcoming 12 months.

An overarching theme in the survey results is that these

adjustments to the compensation offer are highly situational, even if the organization has a policy in place—and nearly one-quarter of survey respondents reported having no specific policy at all.

HIRING BOARD DIRECTORS

It might be a surprise to some, and especially those in executive search firms, that 32% of respondents to our annual Benchmark Survey in 2019 were involved in hiring for board directors at some level, a significant jump from 21% the previous year. Of those 32%, almost half (45%) are doing the searches using their internal recruiters, as opposed to using executive search firms. This is no longer a rare event; it's becoming a mainstream activity.

Having said that, even when board director searches are managed in-house, organizations will often still use a search firm—perhaps to assess the finalist candidate or simply to demonstrate that an external, objective third party was involved in the selection.

In a recent webinar on this topic with several experienced ESIX panelists, we learned a lot about the intricacies of hiring board members:

• Though there is plenty of mystique to board hiring, it's not as complicated as one might think, and in some respects, it's easier than a regular search. Plus, in the normal course of things, it would be unusual to do more than one or two board searches in a year, unless it's a newly created board.

• Typically, we hire a new board member when one of our current board directors "ages out," in other words, is nearing board director age limit. Occasionally, a board member will leave to take a CEO role at a competing organization, or for other reasons becomes unable to fulfill the board role. At other times, an activist investor might instigate a board shake-up.

• There is an unfortunate tendency to hire only sitting or recent CEOs for board roles, which makes hiring diverse board members very difficult. Changing this mindset completely is going to take time. Nevertheless, especially with the influence of some very powerful investors, the pattern is starting to shift. There is a trend toward hiring specialist board members related to specific business strategies, perhaps with "digital" or "consumer" experience, which can broaden the board member pool.

• "Over-boarding," whereby board members might be deemed

to sit on too many boards, is also an issue when hiring board directors. The role may be a challenge for board members whose "day job" is being a CEO who may be unable to give proper attention to the issues of your organization.

For board members without a full-time role, more than two or three board roles might be too many, and for sitting CEOs, one other board seat may be the limit. If one imagines that each board member has to attend at least four multiday board sessions a year, be available for ad hoc and standing committee meetings between times, and take time mentoring company executives, it's easy to see how over-boarding can be a risk. At a tactical level, even board meeting date conflicts can come into play as a deciding factor for potential candidates who sit on more than one board.

• In many cases, board hiring work involves partnering very closely with the General Counsel's office and/or a designated board liaison or compliance officer. It will also involve working with the head of HR as well as the CEO, though the latter to a lesser degree. The General Counsel will often provide a detailed conflict analysis to the board for any serious candidate.

• The search for a board director is a lot like a regular executive search and goes through the same stages—needs analysis, research, identification, outreach, assessment and interviewing— before a final vote of approval. The big difference is that in most board director searches, only one candidate is approached at a time. Only when a candidate turns down the role is another candidate approached. But to avoid delays after a rejection, detailed research should be done before the outreach to identify backup candidates.

The board's governance and/or nominating committees typically handle final assessments, interviews, and selection for recommendation to the nominating committee, which with the CEO will interview candidates.

• Often, the first step in a search is to complete a gap analysis of the board's capabilities and competencies: "What do we need in the future, what do we have today, and therefore how do we fill the gap?"

These capabilities may be industry-related, such as media or healthcare, or functional, such as the need for a sitting CFO or a CIO. Each board committee may also have certain specific needs; for example, a CFO for the finance committee. And the ages of board members will be a factor in board succession plans and the gap analysis.

• There's more stress around a board search than a standard executive search. Many candidates and board members are CEOs who are used to having things done immediately, on demand, while the search process is not always cooperative!

• When an organization uses a search firm for a board search, the fee is traditionally much lower than for an executive search. That's because a board director role is part-time and provides lower compensation than an executive role, and often mostly in stock. In addition, fewer candidates are contacted and less persuasion is needed because, in most cases, candidates do not have to relocate or leave a current role.

• Finally, search firms consider board searches an opportunity. They get to establish or strengthen the client relationship at the highest level and have a reason to contact sitting CEOs or board directors at other organizations, which in itself is a path to potentially more "regular" search work down the line.

ROLE OF THE HR LEADER IN HELPING SEARCHES SUCCEED

As presented by Lucien Alziari, then Division CHRO and VP Talent Management at PepsiCo, now Executive VP and Chief HR Officer, Prudential Financial

Be clear on the need
• Be able to describe success—where the role fits in the organization
• Articulate the difference between the must-haves and the nice-to-haves
• Chart the career path of the position

Own the process
• Nail dates of deliverables and have a clear project plan
• Make sure you are "top-of-search-consultant's-mind"

Maintain momentum
• Keep refining the spec, and keep everything (consultant and hiring team) to a timeline
• Hold search consultants to their commitments
• On diversity, and on hitting candidate qualifications

- Choose initial candidates very carefully—it sets the tone for the rest of the search
- Hold off until a really viable candidate can be presented; good intentions will kill you
- If it's a calibration candidate, make sure everyone understands; first impressions are key

Provide meaningful feedback to search consultants

- Gather "more of/less of" comments to keep refining the spec
- Check how well each stage of the search process is working; is everyone doing their part?
- Remember: The interview is a window on your culture; a challenging experience attracts top talent

Take ownership of top candidates—don't leave them only in the hands of external search consultants

- Build personal relationships
- Let candidates know where they stand
- If you like the candidate, drive for closure
- Stick with the plan, especially when things get tough
- Remind everyone of search goals—avoid the easy option of the internal compromise candidate

Close the deal

- Understand candidates from an early stage; present the proposition in a compelling way
- Look for the emotional leap, but expect moments of tension and demands; know when to walk
- Use the search consultant to test ideas, establish limits, reinforce messages, serve as someone to vent to, and ultimately become an "honest broker"

Manage inside communication very well

- Use senior executives wisely, at the right moment
- Don't use them to negotiate deals
- Never forget that talent really matters
- Find a way to bring them in; do it now
- Can you really have too much talent?

HOW TO DO IT ALL REMOTELY

We recently asked some ESIX members how they have adapted to remote interviewing, hiring, and onboarding. Here is a summary of comments from Adriana Quevedo of Intel; Andy Johnstone of GE Healthcare; Cormac Cullinane of Warner Media; Jackie Morgan of Eaton Corp.; Jess Feller of Verizon; and Juan Calvo of Coca-Cola HBC.

Remote interviewing

The idea that we can hire a senior executive without physically meeting will take time to sink in, but it's becoming a necessary mindset. We learned this and more in a recent ESIX discussion.

For starters, we have to discuss with our hiring teams and with candidates the fact that the entire process could be remote. Not everyone will be immediately comfortable with that, and we need to be flexible and accepting of managers who aren't ready to hire without an elbow bump. Even so, we need to know that before we start the process.

So too some candidates will be uncomfortable making a life-changing decision—not just for them, but also their families—without even seeing their new office building or meeting their prospective colleagues.

Make it clear to each candidate that all candidates are being interviewed by video. Assure them that the meeting background is not important as long as we have a good basic image and sound. For a relaxed setting, you might even suggest casual attire for both candidates and interviewers.

Send technology and logistics details ahead of time, with clear instructions on how to log on and how to set up audio and camera. Ideally, use technology that's browser-centric and doesn't involve a software download.

Also ahead of time, as you would for an in-person interview, send the candidate biographies of the interview team. Talk about the interviewers' style of communication and give guidance on what will be asked and how the various interviews will flow.

During the interview, be aware that when you look away from the screen, it will be more obvious and possibly distracting to the candidate than it would be in person. Mention that you're taking notes for yourself, and also that the candidate's resume is off camera, so that when you do look away, it will be for that reason.

Make sure you're structuring each interview as you would with a series of in-person candidate interviews. Each interviewer should know what's been discussed in previous interviews and should be prepared to explore topics to which they've been assigned.

Remember that time is more limited and that you're missing other elements of the in-person interview: the few minutes in the lobby for the candidate to gather impressions and mentally prepare; the escorted walk to the room from the reception desk; and the escorted exit or transition to another interview.

Some organizations have developed a virtual version of the "white glove walk-in, walk-out" candidate experience, where the recruiter or a coordinator will make sure that all participants are connected and have good audio and video beforehand, help the candidate get settled before the interview begins and then engage the candidate in a post-interview debrief.

Remote hiring

Following second interviews and during the development and delivery of an offer, there's one golden rule: Keep in close contact with the candidate and the hiring manager—especially the candidate. In remote hiring, this is more important than ever. Follow up on every candidate question or concern. Listen for clues to the candidate's state of mind.

If it's an international search, make sure all issues around travel, compensation and benefits, tax laws, immigration, and relocation are being addressed.

Remote onboarding

Just because an executive may be working remotely doesn't mean we can neglect onboarding. In fact, onboarding for remote roles may require an extra level of thoughtfulness and execution. Computers and other work tools should be shipped to the home address before the start date. More tech support than normal will typically be needed. Meeting setups and protocols should be carefully reviewed.

Overcommunication is the idea!

Make sure the new hire's business group has a very interactive plan for them on day one and going forward. Some organizations send the hiring manager a complete package of the candidate assessment, reference notes, and interview notes so they can build a solid onboarding and integration plan.

Introductions are key. The new hire's first week or two might be largely devoted to video calls with each peer, direct report, and manager.

The more structure surrounding the candidate's tasks, performance indicators, and opportunities for success, the better.

WHAT TO DO WHEN THINGS GO AWRY

Not all searches go smoothly, of course. Perhaps it's taking a surprisingly long time to close, or the client is complaining that we're not doing our job well. When a search is in trouble, what next?

First, gather data—which of course we hope you've been collecting all along.

Communication is often the issue in troubled searches, including failure to set proper expectations at the outset. Pull together a document that shows original search parameters, including the top five criteria. Include a complete list of prospects researched and contacted, then a metric of those who responded and the reasons they were rejected, or not interested.

This kind of thorough research will impress a frustrated client. Stark and unfiltered feedback from prospects —especially those who seemed a good match on paper—also helps reset the direction of the search and the client's expectations. While this feedback should not be a surprise at this point, seeing it one report can be striking. Not only does such a report give comfort to the client that you are actually working hard on their behalf, it also gives a reality check on the challenges of the search, and possibly the role itself.

3

SELECTING AND ENGAGING EXECUTIVE SEARCH CONSULTANTS
• • •

HOW SEARCH CONSULTANTS ARE COMPENSATED

When a small group of corporate buyers of executive search services met for the first time in 1996, in what became the ESIX, the first topic they undertook was "How Search Consultants Are Compensated and How That Affects Client Service." As they found—and as a rule of thumb this remains in effect—consultants typically receive about half of their "billings" (i.e., revenues received from clients they have served over the course of the year).

If a consultant establishes the opportunity to pitch a search to a client, confirms the search in a letter of engagement, and executes the search to the client's satisfaction, then they are credited with earning the entire fee minus whatever the search firm withholds to cover its expenses. Again, the consultant is likely to receive about half of the fee while the search firm keeps about half. This breakdown varies by firm and is often adjusted to provide an even higher percentage of billings to top performers.

It gets more interesting when more than one consultant or associate is involved—which happens often, if not most of the time. Then, fee billings are shared based on who was responsible for which part(s) of the process. Typically, about half of the fee billings (and sometimes more) go to the consultant who "sold" the search, which again can be shared if one consultant established the opportunity and another achieved the actual sale of the engagement. The other half (and sometimes less) goes to the consultant and/or associate who executed the search.

This is what gets the attention of clients and creates what you might consider a conflict: The aim of the search firm is to grow the firm, so it tends to reward the "sell" of the engagement, while the aim of the client is outstanding execution of the search. Clients would like to see a greater share of fees going to the folks who actually get the job done.

It's worth exploring in your discussions with search consultants.

SEARCH FEES AND EXPENSES

Good executive search consultants earn good money. Great search consultants earn great money. There are several reasons:

- Top consultants are typically advanced in their careers, hold graduate degrees (often MBAs), have significant executive-level experience, have spent years building networks of sources in their industry and/or function, and are skilled in selling to both clients and candidates.
- For most hiring organizations, a senior-level search is an occasional event, which means search consultants spend quite a bit of time positioning themselves for those occasions—getting to know clients and making proposals that may or may not result in a search.
- A search consultant can handle several searches simultaneously if they are not all at the same stage, but this requires the strong support of a researcher and/or administrative assistant.
- When a consultant engages and completes a search with a terrific candidate, the positive impact on an organization is significant. Some say executive search is the most valuable kind of management consulting.

As a consequence, fees are high. If you broke it down by the hour, it might look like what a lawyer or management consultant would charge.

But rather than simply charging by the hour, search consultants foresaw a more lucrative opportunity. In the years after World War II, they began to charge a fee based on the compensation of the hired candidate. The bigger the job, the higher the fee. In early years, that fee was about 15% of a hired candidate's guaranteed annual compensation. It ratcheted up to 25%, then 30%, and finally in the 1980s reached the limit of what the market would bear: 33%.

More recently, advances in technology, the expanded competitiveness of the executive search industry and pressures on fees from corporate cost management have lowered that percentage closer to 30%. It's still a lot of money, especially in light of how compensation packages have grown over the years.

RETAINED VS. CONTINGENCY

When considering executive recruiters, there are two flavors: retained and contingency. Retained firms charge a fee to conduct a search, regardless of the outcome. Contingency firms send you an invoice only when you hire someone.

It sounds like a simple difference in how the recruiter is paid, but it's amplified in how the work is carried out.

A retained firm, assured of being paid, assigns resources necessary to carry out a process through which the client can hire the best person available—regardless of how long it takes. A contingency firm, lacking this assurance, has to take its chances—that is, limit the investment of time in any particular search because a successful outcome depends on factors beyond the recruiter's control.

Contingency recruiters typically work with a large number of job openings. Using a database of known candidates, they look for matches on paper and send as many resumes as possible to the client for possible interviews. As such, the contingency process is geared to identifying qualified candidates—but not necessarily the most qualified candidates who could be found if significant research and in-person interviewing were applied to the hiring organization's particular need.

Contingency recruiting is appropriate in the following situations:
- When the salary level is at the lower end of your executive population
- When many people are likely to be qualified for the position
- When multiple positions with the same job description are being filled
- When the hiring organization wants to take more responsibility for screening, interviewing, and negotiating with candidates

Retained search is appropriate when the hiring organization wants to:
- Fill a role in the upper echelons of the executive population
- Engage a consultant to make a dedicated effort on its behalf, including persuading top candidates to consider the opportunity and to negotiate the terms of the move
- Hire not just a qualified person, but the most qualified person available

- Use an independent third party to thoroughly screen candidates through in-person interviews before finalists are presented
- Evaluate internal candidates as well as externals
- Approach potential candidates on a confidential basis

And so we find that retained consultants typically work exclusively on any given search and are expected to evaluate all candidates being considered. As a result, a retained consultant will (almost) never present a candidate to more than one client at a time. A contingency recruiter usually does not have an exclusive assignment but instead is in a race against other sources to present a winning candidate. Contingency recruiters often present attractive candidates to as many clients as possible.

Contingency recruiters also tend to be more specialized by industry and function, while retained search consultants also specialize but can also apply an original-research approach across industries.

HOW TO STRUCTURE THE FEE

Despite the differences in the two models described above, clients do not always have to make an "either/or" decision. As you might imagine, there's a middle ground—that is, a retained search mindset combined with an element of a contingency fee structure, sometimes called "retingency" or "container." Under this arrangement, part of the fee is paid to initiate the search and the rest is contingent on hiring.

It's a popular approach and the result of buyers wanting the search firm to have "skin in the game." But many search firms resist such contracts, as they can't control whether an organization makes a hire. When a search firm performs as promised, why should it forgo part of the fee if the client changes plans or simply moves slowly?

Meanwhile, companies need to think carefully about the downside of making the final search firm payment contingent on hiring. It gives the search consultant an excuse to quit working on the engagement if the consultant comes to believe that a hire is just not going to happen. This removes the leverage clients have under a fully retained structure, where the search consultant is obligated to continue working on the engagement until the client is satisfied.

To address the issue, some companies have opted instead for payments based on milestones that both parties can commit to.

Here's one model: First payment on initiation, second payment on scheduling of the first qualified candidate(s) for an interview (organization can cancel before second payment with no penalty); third payment on resolution of the search, which can be either a placement or a decision to close the search. While this more or less guarantees a full fee to the search firm, at least the fee is not fully paid before the work is done.

An even simpler model is: First third of the fee on initiation, second third on presentation of a slate of candidates, third payment after 60, or sometimes 90, days. A variation on that is to tie the third payment to the client's decision to see a candidate for a second time.

Finally, there's the option of stepping away from percentage fees entirely and paying for search on an hourly basis. Few retained search firms do this, however.

Fixed fees

When clients seek more control over the fee structure, a popular approach is to use a set fee based on a percentage of projected compensation but nevertheless fixed in advance. For example, if, in developing the position specification, the hiring team and search consultant can agree on an anticipated guaranteed annual compensation for the role, the search fee can be fixed to an amount based on a percentage of that compensation. Let's say we agree on 30% and the projected compensation is US$400K. The search fee can then be set at US$120K—and by the way, we'd like that to include all expenses except candidate travel.

A fixed fee has several advantages:
• It forces an honest conversation between the search consultant and the hiring team on what the projected compensation is likely to be. This helps to avoid a common pitfall: engaging in a search where the client has a compensation point in mind while the search consultant secretly knows that the right candidate will cost more than that. (Searches sometimes fail for this reason.) When the search fee is going to be fixed, the search consultant must be forthright about what compensation will actually be required.
• It removes any interest, real or perceived, that the search consultant may have in maximizing the compensation in order to maximize the search fee.
• It avoids an unnecessary discussion that often takes place when percentage fees are used: On what number will we calculate the percentage fee? Will it include the sign-on bonus? Stock? Relocation? When complex compensation packages are being

negotiated, it's a distraction to have to also negotiate the search fee.

• It allows the hiring organization to plan ahead for the final cost of the search.

More ideas

Isn't there an even better way? Corporate executive search leaders tossed this around recently and came up with the following suggestions that come roughly under the heading, "A better fee structure would include …"

• **Fixed fees by compensation bracket**, such as a US$50K fixed fee for positions up to US$150K total compensation; US$60K for jobs paying US$150K–US$200K; US$75K for jobs paying US$200K–US$300K; and US$25K for every US$100K in compensation above that, up to a cap of, say, US$300K.

• **Hourly pricing** of unbundled services, such as research only or assessment only.

• **Graduated hourly rates by task**, such as US$250/hour for research (100 hours?), US$350/hour for assessment (50 hours?), and US$500/hour for closing (25 hours?), with a US$10K kicker on completion (total in this example US$65K). The idea is that if it can be done in less time, it will cost less.

• An **"exclusive contingency"** arrangement in which the search firm is engaged on an exclusive basis but most or all of the fee is paid on hiring.

• **Split engagements**, in which a research fee (say US$50K) is paid up front and, if results indicate going forward, a second payment is made to complete the search.

• **Pipeline pricing**, or quarterly payments for discovering and presenting candidates to fill ongoing executive-level needs, with success fees paid when hires result.

• **Less up front**, such as 10% of the fee to initiate, 10% midway through the search, and 80% on hiring.

• **Longer payouts**. Instead of fees billed at initiation, after 30 days and after 60 days, paying out at initiation, 45 days and 90 days; or initiation, at presentation of candidates for interviews, and upon acceptance of an offer.

• **More tradeoffs**, such as getting appropriate credit for canceled searches, and bigger breaks on second and third hires from an initial search.

• **Some way to find value not tied to compensation**, and to reward relationships instead of transactions.

EXPENSES

Taking a cue from attorneys, executive search consultants bill clients for expenses connected to their searches. It's normal and to be expected that clients will reimburse search firms for the costs of candidate travel and other significant expenses incurred by the search firm in the course of a search and directly attributable to each search. These expenses should be approved in advance and itemized in invoices to clients.

In addition, the largest retained search firms, and some smaller ones, charge clients an additional "administrative surcharge" that is meant to cover general expenses, not itemized and not specific to individual searches. The administrative surcharge can be as much as 12% of the fee—not exactly pocket change, but in fact thousands of dollars, again on top of out-of-pocket costs that can be attributed to the search at hand.

Here, clients can argue that they should not be responsible for the search firm's general expenses. The surcharge is a point of contention and one that can be negotiated, if the search firm is sufficiently motivated. Clients deemed "important" by volume of activity or the search firm's desire to continue to serve the client are often able to reduce or even eliminate the administrative surcharge.

In the annual ESIX Benchmark Survey of 90 large companies, just over half of respondents pay administrative expenses, and those who do pay an average of 6.9% of the fee if it is based on a percentage of the hired candidate's compensation. If the client is paying the search firm on a fixed fee, the average is 3% of the fee, or US$5,475 based on an average fee of US$177K.

As clients have become more insistent on avoiding the administrative surcharge, these figures have declined in recent years to a point where we wonder whether the entire concept is on its last legs.

HOW TO SELECT A SEARCH CONSULTANT

Before even thinking about managing leadership recruiting as a corporate initiative, and probably before you seek to establish an in-house search function, you must know how to pick the right external search consultant for specific needs. And you need to engage and advise hiring managers in that process, since many HR and line managers select search consultants with little or no useful guidance on how to do it well.

Here's what we need to know about search consultants. Typically, most of this information is gathered, in writing, in advance of an in-person discussion:

- The individual consultant's performance record at our organization and/or elsewhere
- Specific individual and firm strengths in the function and industry at hand
- The opportunity for a good fit between the search consultant and potential candidates (i.e., a background and an approach that will help attract top candidates)
- The opportunity for a good working relationship with the hiring executive
- In cases where wide-ranging markets will be searched, resources equal to the task—experienced consultants in appropriate locations for international searches (Key here is the ability of the search firm to function effectively with partners who may not be highly motivated to participate fully in an engagement originating outside their home office.)
- Who will be chiefly responsible for the relationship with the organization and how the firm will staff the project (Who will do the research? Who will develop candidates? Who will interview? Who will check references?)
- How quickly the search can be completed (performance records are helpful)
- What fees and expenses would be charged, and how they would be billed
- What guarantees are available to replace a hired executive who doesn't work out
- The consultant's record of recruiting diverse candidates
- How reference checks are handled
- Ability and experience in evaluating inside candidates (if applicable)

Armed with this knowledge, we're now ready to have a conversation with the consultant that will give us a better idea of how things might go. You'll want to pose new questions and follow up on others by asking:

- *What searches have you conducted <u>personally</u> that are relevant to the prospective engagement, and when were they completed?*
Here we want to make sure that the consultant is not simply reciting projects that others in the firm conducted.

- *What searches are you working on currently, and where do they stand?*
We especially want to know about any searches that could be drawing from a candidate pool similar to ours. And we need a sense of the consultant's workload. A handful of current engagements is okay as long as they are not all bunched at the intense initial stages. Keep asking until you get a satisfactory answer (which always seems to be four or five).

- *Please describe a recent search similar to ours that went well, and one that didn't go well.*
The consultant should have no trouble with the former, while the latter offers an opportunity for candor—or obfuscation.

- *What has been the compensation range of searches you have conducted in the past year?*
We want to know that the consultant works regularly at the level of your search.

- *What other searches like this is your firm working on?*
Even if there's no direct conflict, we want to know if there may be competition for candidates within the search firm.

- *How does your firm decide which candidates will be presented to which client?*
Another opportunity for candor, or not, about how the search firm operates.

- *Which companies would be targeted?*
Executive Search 101: The consultant should be well prepared to answer this question at the outset.

- *Which companies, or parts of companies, would not be approached due to client obligations?*
Again, disclosure is the mark of professionalism. Sometimes, it's necessary to keep asking, "And where else would you not be

comfortable looking?"

• *How would you describe our organization to candidates?*
The answer here will provide insight into whether the consultant has done the homework.

• *How would candidates be identified, qualified, and described before presentation?*
A chance to learn more about who does what and how they do it.

• *How would candidates be assessed for management style and cultural fit?*
We want a solid understanding of the consultant's capabilities on these vital issues and to what extent they're familiar with the culture of the hiring organization.

• *What would you do to surface diverse candidates?*
Ideally, the consultant is full of specific ideas and tactics.

• *When will references be checked, and how will this be reported?*
An opportunity to make sure this base is well covered.

• *What compensation will be required to attract the successful candidate?*
Agreement on this point is essential to a successful outcome.

• *What would be the most likely causes for failure in this search?*
You may get a throwaway line here—but you may also get something really insightful.

SEARCH FIRM SELECTION CRITERIA

Once search consultants have been interviewed and proposals have been solicited, search consultants can be scored on whatever criteria apply best to the specific engagement. For almost any search, the following six criteria can be used— and can be easily remembered by the acronym **SEARCH**:

S   Successful work for us and/or others. The key criterion is a past record of success in serving our organization, primarily, and/or others where we have checked references.

E   Experience relevant to the engagement at hand. Whether for us or for other clients, it's important that the consultant has done work at this level that's very similar, even if not exactly like it (since every search is unique).

A   Access to potential candidates at target companies. We need to ensure not only that the search consultant has the resources to cast a wide net but also is not blocked by other client relationships from approaching individuals at targeted companies.

R   Responsiveness. The search firm's communication style— which is key to successful search work—becomes evident in the process of considering them for each assignment. How crisp and complete are they in communicating with us so far?

C   Capacity. Does the selected individual consultant have time not only to conduct the search but also to give us any extra attention we may need to achieve success? Is the consultant's capacity free of conflict from competing searches? Does the firm have resources appropriate to the engagement?

H   How much is the fee? Cost should be strictly secondary to using the best consultant but can be a tiebreaker between two who are equally qualified. And is the selected search firm comfortable with all of our terms of engagement?

THE ENGAGEMENT LETTER

Once a search consultant has been selected, it's paramount—we mean that this is the most important step a client can take in launching a search—to formalize the agreement in an engagement letter that spells out what's going to happen and who's responsible. It's typical for the search firm to generate such a letter, or contract, to suit its desires and conditions. Here is the moment where you, the hiring organization, can step up and present your terms to which you seek the search firm's commitment.

It's in everyone's interest to understand expectations. In Chapter 7, we offer a template for an engagement letter. Here, we want to describe what it should cover, along with specific suggestions on what the terms might be.

Who's involved	Name all participants and describe their roles (search consultant, any assistants, hiring executive, and all members of hiring team).
Fees	Will be fixed in advance at a percentage of the successful candidate's anticipated first-year total cash compensation (not including sign-on/relocation payments).
Expenses	Will be included except for candidate and consultant travel, which will be incurred with advance approval and itemized in invoices to the client organization.
Invoicing	Often takes place over three months, with each invoice based on a mutually agreed milestone.
Cancellation	Note what part of the fee will be paid if the search is canceled, for example: one-third of the fee if canceled during the first month; two-thirds of the fee if canceled during the second month; three-quarters of the fee if canceled during the third month; a full fee thereafter.
Additional hires	The fee for an additional hire made within one year from among candidates presented in full resume format (at minimum) by the search consultant will be, for example, 20% of anticipated first-year total cash compensation.
Exclusivity	Note that the search firm is working exclusively on the engagement. All candidates will be referred to the firm regardless of where they originate from.

Process	The firm will follow the Code of Ethics and Professional Practice Guidelines of the Association of Executive Search and Leadership Consultants.
Equal opportunity	That the search firm will document efforts to identify and recruit candidates of all backgrounds, without regard to race, gender, age, or other factors unrelated to their ability to perform in the position.
Target dates	Include a schedule for the steps in the process by which both parties can measure progress during the search.
Client's role	Commit to availability for communication and interviews.
Change of spec	Make provision for additional fees if a significant change of specification occurs during the search.
Guarantee	Note that if the hired candidate leaves the organization within the first year, the search firm will search for a replacement at no fee (expenses only).
Off-limits	The search firm will refrain from recruiting individuals from the client organization, or a unit of such, for a specified period of time following the search.

ON MEASURING SEARCH FIRM PERFORMANCE

Executive search consulting has two elements:
• Using research and assessment to find and recruit individuals who meet specific criteria

- Helping organizations make good plans and decisions before, during and after hiring

The first applies to all recruiting; the second applies only to retained search consulting. The first can be quantified; the second resists measurement. The first is a transaction; the second reflects a relationship. The first is a science; the second is an art.

These contrasts provide the challenge in developing programs for the use of executive search consultants. In fact, the whole idea of having "a program" for the selection and use of search consultants is at odds with the consultative side of executive search. Still, the results side of search cries out for measurement and analysis.

Our thesis
1. Historically, relationships between search consultants and companies have developed on a random basis, reflecting the relationship side of executive search.
2. Introducing some science into the process of selecting and using search firms can bring a needed balance to the intangible aspects of the recruiting process.
3. Through a balanced approach, it's possible that cost, speed, and quality can be improved simultaneously.

What and how to measure
Cost savings are easily measured, and some can be achieved simply by paying attention to the process of engaging firms. Second, there's an opportunity to gain speed by using search consultants most knowledgeable in relevant markets and by developing deeper relationships with selected consultants. They begin to know the organization better by virtue of representing it regularly—thereby saving time in the critical first several weeks of a search.

How do we define and measure quality? There are actually two kinds of quality that are important here: the quality of service provided by the consultant and the quality of candidates presented.

Quality of service is reflected in responsiveness, dependability, and evidence of hard work in conducting the search engagement—all of which can be tracked in post-search surveys. In theory, corporate efforts to strengthen search firm relationships help improve the quality of search services, because the consultants get to know the organization better and can invest to a greater extent in being responsive. Ultimately, this may also translate into higher-quality candidates being developed and presented.

But the quality of candidates is the most difficult-to-measure aspect of executive search. Actual long-term performance of hired candidates is the best measure, but by the time this becomes known, circumstances surrounding search firm selection for new engagements will have changed.

One interesting suggestion for measuring candidate quality is to record "yield"—the number of candidates presented before an offer is extended. While this number should never get lower than three or so, if it's 15 or 20, then there's a problem with candidate quality. ESIX benchmark surveys show companies that manage and measure executive recruiting activity average five to six presented candidates per hire.

In sum, the goal is to develop a program that blends strategic sourcing with the intangibles of relationship-building that together are core of success in leadership recruiting.

MYTHBUSTING

We must say there are rumors about search consultants that deserve dispelling. For example:

Search consultants just tap their databases to find great candidates. The days of search consultant Rolodexes are long gone, thanks to the internet and good executive search management by corporations. In fact, the value of search firms is now more in the consulting and assessing, rather than in the discovery of candidates.

Having said that, thanks to their extensive databases and constant activity in the market, executive search resources and relationships are still quite useful.

You can't trust search firms.

On the contrary, the more the search firm knows about the organization, the hiring manager, the competition, and the risks and challenges of hiring, the more it can be a true partner—and the less time the search will take. Start relationships with an open, trusting mindset if possible.

Meanwhile, trust but verify. Set clear expectations; make sure all stakeholders understand the urgency of the hiring need. Then monitor the search firm closely to ensure action is being taken between each update call.

Search consultants should know all the candidate's compensation data in the first call.

Not so much. It's like dating: You don't often get the shoe size and blood type of your date at the first dinner. We're talking about prospects you are courting and persuading away from their current "steady." Further, changes in the law (in some regions) aimed at reducing gender discrimination require that we avoid gathering compensation history and focus instead on compensation expectations.

Search firms push for higher compensation to get higher fees.

In fact, there is no real data to show this is true. If you've done your homework, know the market, and know the candidate, then you know what the right price really is. Search firms have much more to lose by souring a corporate relationship than by gaining a few thousand more on one search.

TOP 10 ETHICAL CHALLENGES IN EXECUTIVE SEARCH

10. Representing the service faithfully: Are they conducting searches or floating resumes?

9. Maintaining loyalty to clients amid complex client relationships and tactics (double-teaming)

8. Disclosing investments or other interests in potential target companies

7. Treating candidates fairly

6. Avoiding being used as a tool to discriminate against qualified candidates

5. Using the search process to advance diversity—and avoid reverse discrimination

4. Fully disclosing all constraints: Off-limits; competing searches; investments/alliances

3. Being honest about the purpose of initial calls to potential candidates

2. Respecting sources of information: Ownership of research; copyrights; sharing proprietary info; taking data home, or to your new job

1. Maintaining confidentiality around client and candidate information

True story: In the middle of a high-profile CEO search, a search consultant is overheard on an airplane discussing a candidate. It gets back to candidate's boss, who threatens to fire the candidate. Outcome:

Search firm completes the search but loses the new CEO's confidence and therefore the account.

Given the increased awareness about personal data and privacy nowadays, particularly in the age of General Data Protection Regulation (GDPR) in Europe and similar regulations elsewhere, this is an area that deserves more scrutiny in both the corporate and the search firm world. In fact, we recently heard of one case where a candidate had submitted their resume to a recruitment firm in the UK and instructed the firm to send it to only four companies. The recruitment firm sent the resume to an additional company, which called the candidate directly. The candidate was very upset and contacted the UK GDPR regulator, which gave the recruitment firm a warning. This could have been much worse for the recruitment firm, as they could have been fined up to 4% of revenues. And this regulation applies to corporate recruiting groups too.

HOW TO QUERY A SEARCH FIRM ON ETHICS

David Moyer, of New York–based search firm Moyer, Sherwood Associates, is a student of ethics in executive recruiting and has served on the Ethics Committee of the Association of Executive Search and Leadership Consultants (AESC). He offers the following comments:

Checking out the degree of thought around ethics gives you insight into the character of search consultants. It could make a big difference in the firm's performance of the search, and its outcome.

It's easy for a search consultant to nod reassuringly when the subject of ethics and professional practices comes up. Any decent consultant will be able to talk about their firm's approach to frequently raised questions such as off-limits restrictions and conflicts of interest. So how can you ferret out what a search consultant really thinks about ethics, and predict who's paying attention to this critical area and who's just paying it lip service?

Start with the AESC's guidelines, available online at www.aesc.org. If the search firm you're talking to raises the subject, that's a good sign. Find out if they are aware of and follow AESC guidelines. Consider insisting in the engagement letter that the firm abide by these guidelines regardless of whether it belongs to the association. The association can't take any action against non-member firms for breaches of ethics, but at least you'll have the AESC Code as a benchmark.

Then, try to launch a discussion about a few of the Code's provisions. Here are questions with no specific desired responses or "right answers." Instead you simply want evidence that the consultant has considered the issues and, ideally, is familiar enough with the Code to be able to discuss them spontaneously:

What ethical point is most absolute to you? Which is the softest, most fluid, subject to change?

While there's no single right answer, "objectivity" and "integrity" are likely responses to the first question. The second is the harder to answer, but "public interest" is an area in which thoughtful, honest consultants may have genuine differences, and respecting confidential information entrusted to them by candidates can legitimately conflict with ethical responsibilities to clients.

Tell me about a search you declined.

A good search firm should turn down assignments here and there. One good reason might be that two assignments are too similar. But it would be valid to say simply that they didn't have capacity to handle workload beyond a certain point. You want search firms to bite off only what they can chew.

Has an ethical issue caused you to resign a search in mid-assignment?

This is a hard thing to do, so if the answer is no, you can ask for an example of a situation where in retrospect they wish they had … and watch for a knowing sigh. Every search consultant with substantial experience who's serious about ethics has at least one regret in this area.

It's also tough to talk to a potential client about, since client error can be the precipitating factor. A good example might be a client who sought "back-door" references on a candidate without talking to the search firm about confidentiality. A client who deliberately misleads candidates about responsibilities or seriously understates internal politics to finalists could be other examples.

How do you train your people in this area?

Large firms have full-blown training programs. At a small firm, it might be as simple as pairing a new consultant with a senior partner who has special interest in ethics. The person you're talking to might tell you of their experience when joining the firm, how structured or loose the training was then, and how it's changed in the X years since. Again, what you're looking for are details that support credibility rather than pat responses or vague generalities.

What's different about how a business service is provided and a professional service?

As an HR professional about to authorize a considerable

expenditure of your corporation's money, you may want to hear from your "vendor" that "the customer is always right." With an ethical retained search firm, however, you're much better off with one who knows the difference between customers and clients and who establishes the relationship of a partner with you—free to disagree on the way to a solution. This question may stimulate a productive conversation about just that approach.

Probing these issues elevates the level of your relationship with the search consultant. Just having the conversation sends a signal to the search firm that you and your corporation take these concerns seriously and that you expect them to play by the rules.

We talk about a lot of factors during engagement meetings and shoot-outs. Devoting time to ethics and professionalism treats ethics as a muscle, one that remains strong and effective only with exercise. Hopefully, these questions will act as your gym.

● ● ●

"On a CEO search, a search firm presented long list of candidates that included an individual our Chair knew to have passed away more than 18 months earlier. The search firm's assertion that they had spoken with the candidate 'relatively recently' caused us to consider finding another search partner. But after considerable debate, we decided to continue working with the search firm and, to be sure, the search went very smoothly thereafter." **– ELIZABETH WALLACE, HEAD OF PORTFOLIO TALENT, Hg**

SEARCH FIRM REFERENCE QUESTIONS

Stephen Bianchi, former Senior Executive Recruiter at Vanguard, suggests the following format for gathering references on an executive search firm from past or present clients.

Reference Name and Title:
Reference Contact Information:
Date:
RE: (Search Firm Name)

- What search(es) has (Search Firm) completed for you in the last 12 months and/or what active searches are under way with your organization?

• If you had an upcoming search, would you put (Search Firm) into the short list for firms that would potentially be awarded the search?

• Who is your primary point of contact at (Search Firm)?

• Describe the firm's effectiveness in following organization process.

• Describe the reach of the firm. Did they cover the market and provide a deep pool of candidates?

• Did the firm bring you a pool of candidates that had both gender and minority representation?

• Describe their knowledge of the market. Can they differentiate the best candidates and were their candidate submissions on point?

• Have they learned the culture of your firm and therefore represented your organization effectively?

• Did they do a good job with reporting requests and accuracy of candidate information?

• Are they good at selecting talent? Do they follow any particular interview methodology?

• What does their track record look like? Do candidates stick and perform well?

• Are they easy to work with? Good at listening? Flexible as the search evolves?

• Did you ever sense that they were over capacity and not able to provide the needed resources?

• What aspects if any related to the search assignment that you would have liked (Search Firm) to approach in a different fashion?

• Did any issues of ethics or integrity arise in the course of your work with the firm?

• Any open commentary that you would like to add?

OFF-LIMITS: THE PRICE OF PROTECTION

Among issues in executive recruiting that never go away is off-limits—the agreement by search providers to refrain from recruiting your executives to the search firm's other clients. In general, there's been erosion of support for the concept. As search firms have grown and consolidated, creating longer and longer client rosters, and developed additional lines of services, they've sought to narrow the scope of off-limits protection granted to any given client. To do otherwise would shrink the territory in which they can search to a point of ineffectiveness. Competition for leadership talent only exacerbates the issue.

In ESIX surveys, participants have been divided. While many major, mature, and highly principled organizations continue to feel that they shouldn't use search firms that are likely to accept fees with one hand and extract talent from the organization with the other ... some more aggressive and pragmatic companies are willing to play a more open game in which they get greater access to the talent market in exchange for giving up insistence on a comprehensive off-limits guarantee for themselves.

Meanwhile, some companies get around this tradeoff by using small search firms, for whom off-limits for a handful of clients is not a problem.

But for those unwilling to give up on the idea that some kind of off-limits protection is still an important consideration in relationships with large search firms, questions remain:

- What scope of protection makes sense in today's market?
- To what extent should it be tied to the amount of work the search firm is doing for you?
- What does it really take to get worldwide protection from a global search firm these days?

In our experience at the Executive Search Information Exchange, we have seen that several participating organizations have succeeded in obtaining worldwide off-limits protection from major search firms without committing to a specific amount of work that would go to the search firm over the course of a relationship agreement with the firm. Several others have obtained global protection by committing to a certain amount of work from the search firm. The amount of work an organization typically commits to in order to receive global protection from a major search firm varies according to the level of search activity and on the size of the client.

Geographic issues plague these relationships. Search firms get work in one part of the world but not others, putting severe pressure on the search firm to maintain off-limits protection in parts of the world where the firm isn't getting any—or enough—work. For this reason, the scope of off-limits protection is limited to business units or geographical areas for many ESIX participants.

Where are the penalties for violating off-limits?

When an executive search firm violates an off-limits agreement, should it pay a penalty?

Common sense seems to say yes. The idea that a professional services firm must refrain from soliciting client employees for jobs elsewhere is fundamental to the search firm-client relationship. It should not be difficult to honor. Surprisingly, however, more than one-third of ESIX companies surveyed at one point had no specified penalty, or even a stated consequence, for violations of off-limits agreements.

This is not to say companies don't have strong feelings about this state of affairs. A solid 65% say an off-limits violation typically results in termination of the relationship. Some use harsh language: "A public flogging"; "... angry phone calls"; "We would notify all hiring executives in writing, explain the blatant disregard for professionalism and create a blacklist."

But many are conflicted: "We have different legal views"; "... not clearly defined"; "... hard to enforce, hard to know"; "We would terminate the relationship; however, it's difficult to manage in a global organization"; "We certainly would not bring legal action unless there is a substantial case to be won and we can demonstrate they had access to information that they used inappropriately."

Only seven of 40 companies surveyed were likely to consider an actual financial penalty, and even then, specified penalties typically fall short of requiring the search firm to pay damages. Among the seven, one said it would be "credit to us for the cost of the search," which raises the question of how that credit would be used if the search firm no longer does business with the organization.

Another said that even though "it goes without saying that we would take some sort of legal action ... we have nothing built into our contracts." Two others said penalties are not automatic. "We may demand a refund or something of the like," said one, while the other said, "We may look at legal remedies and see fee reimbursement."

Only two companies offered language in their contracts that sets up the issue of damages. One company warns the search firm that if it breaches the off-limits provision, it is agreeing in advance that the client will have suffered "irreparable harm" and be entitled "to seek injunctive relief ... without having to prove damages or post a bond."

The second offers this:

> If Agency hires, recruits or assists another in hiring an employee of X, then Agency shall pay to X liquidated damages to cover X's costs related to replacing such personnel, loss of

services, opportunity costs, impact on current and future projects and the like (and) one year of the hired employee's annual salary in lump sum payment within 2 weeks of the date upon which the employee leaves their employment at X. Liquidated damages shall not limit or impair any other remedies that X may seek for breach of this section of the agreement.

However, only one of the 40 companies stated that it had actually collected damages resulting from breach of an off-limits agreement; in that case, restitution of the US$149K fee earned for the search that resulted in the off-limits violation.

In fact, the survey was prompted by this very problem. It was suggested by an ESIX participant in the midst of negotiations with a major search firm over the off-limits provision in the firm's contract. The organization was seeking to establish a penalty for off-limits violations equal to one-half of the starting compensation of the individual recruited in violation of the agreement. In other words, the penalty would be somewhat higher than the fee earned (up to one-third of compensation), making it more expensive for the search firm to break the off-limits agreement than to abide by it.

But the search firm argued that the penalty should be only one-third of compensation.

That a search firm can take such an approach to an issue that virtually defines client loyalty is evidence of the apparent lack of interest among companies in holding search firms to this basic principle of professionalism.

Do senior executives still secretly see search firms as possible agents for their own careers and so don't want to punish them for the occasional raid?

Perhaps search firms occasionally see the end of a relationship in sight and decide to trade the easy opportunity of an immediate fee for the uncertain prospects of a stagnant relationship. Or, more frightening: Are search firms simply getting away with off-limits violations such a high percentage of the time—because we aren't checking—that they find the risk acceptable?

Most participants say they have not had to confront the issue. Let's hope it isn't because they aren't looking.

Scope and duration of off-limits agreements

How much off-limits protection do organizations actually get?

Not that long ago, two years was the standard length of off-limits protection granted by the better retained search firms. Today, one year is the rule, and in many cases, the scope of the protection is very limited: sometimes just the hiring manager and direct reports, but more often the department or function. A large organization would have to be spending multiple millions of dollars in fees with a leading search firm to obtain global protection these days. But some do, and global protection is the third-most-common policy among ESIX survey respondents.

Off-limits has always been a tough issue to negotiate, perhaps partly because it seems it shouldn't have to be negotiated at all: You're either a client, or you're not. But failure to address it—with penalties that show search firms you mean business—leaves companies vulnerable rather than protected.

ON THE DISCLOSURE OF SEARCH RESEARCH

Let's say a US$2B consumer goods manufacturer begins searching for a CEO in March, using a leading international search firm. By October, no hire has occurred. Four candidates have reached second interviews but have fallen out for reasons having to do with compensation, the organization's industry, and its location.

Members of the board's search committee are highly frustrated with the lack of success, and a perceived lack of effort by the search firm. They ask for information to help them understand where the search consultants have looked and what they have found. The search firm provides a list of several hundred job titles and organization names, but no information about contacts made and outcomes. The client repeats its request for information to substantiate contact with prospective candidates and receives only a one-paragraph summary offering general reasons why candidates contacted have not been interested in the position.

What information is a client entitled to receive as part of a retained search engagement?

Search firms say candidate confidentiality is endangered when specific contacts are disclosed. Search firms also say their sources are proprietary—not the client's property. Meanwhile, when clients purchase search research independently, they receive detailed information on prospective candidates as part of the work product.

We can reasonably conclude that candidate confidentiality can be endangered through unprofessional handling of search research information, but this alone is not sufficient reason to withhold all information—especially when the client seeks substantiation of efforts to reach prospective candidates. We would therefore propose that executive search consultants should substantiate their work and document candidate research by providing detailed information—verbally or in writing—on prospective candidates contacted and the outcome of those contacts.

HOW TO STRUCTURE AN INTERNATIONAL SEARCH

Multinational organizations regularly need to recruit executives far from corporate headquarters, even though the positions often report to the home office. Achieving high success rates in such searches is a continuing challenge to heads of executive recruiting.

This gives rise to a number of questions: Should we build global partnerships with global search firms to address these needs? Or should they be addressed case-by-case? Can we build an in-house capability? Or should we work with a consultant who knows us well here, hoping that effective research can be done in the distant market? Or should we go straight to a local search firm?

Some organizations do enough international recruiting that it makes sense to develop an in-house search team that can function globally, with outposts in key locations. But most companies are limited to using external search providers. In that context, options are:

- Local independent search firm
- Local office of an international search firm or network
- Domestic consultant who knows your organization and can work with a distant local office

Criteria:

What's the level of the search? Do you need the prestige, reach, or comfort level of a big-name search firm? This may be useful when looking for a regional or country head but not for a head of function or other mid-management role. Furthermore, a recognized brand in your country may not have the same cachet in another region.

Where are the decision-makers based? Will they need the comfort level of having a consultant who knows them and the organization well?

How familiar are the decision-makers with the country/region? If they know the market well, they'll be better able to assess candidates themselves and less reliant on local support. If they are unfamiliar with the market, a savvy consultant will be all the more valuable in helping make an informed decision.

Will you be looking for candidates both at home and abroad? If so, it makes sense to have a search provider with domestic-based research and interviewers.

How wide will the geographic net be spread? The search provider should be able to search across regional and country borders. Most Western Europe–based recruiters are able to search throughout Europe and may have experience in parts of Asia and in North America.

If you are looking to hire internationally, bear in mind that local search firms may be hampered by geopolitical constraints. For instance, local recruiters in China may not want to search in Japan and vice versa, because of historic and cultural sensitivities. Similar issues can be found in some countries in Latin America. The Middle East is another sensitive area.

Yet local firms also have advantages. Too often, non-local search consultants take on an overseas search without researching the basics of language and regional cultural issues.

Will you be looking inside the country only, or will you look within the region? If it's a regional role, or the local candidate pool is limited, you'll need to broaden the search. In doing so, make sure your consultant has the necessary reach. Searches may need to be expanded as feedback from the market comes in.

More to consider:

- Local consultants can often find "hidden" candidates not visible to those unfamiliar with the local market.
- But in smaller markets, candidate blockages (off-limits) may be a big issue. Your target list probably includes companies in a local consultant's current or potential client base.
- Multinational search firms may have excellent consultants in major offices but may not be as strong or consistent throughout their network of affiliate or branch offices. Some local offices are independent profit centers where control and central authority is weak.
- Your local organization manager may be able to maintain good communication with a local search firm. But the local consultant may not communicate well across time differences, geographic constraints and cultural and language barriers.
- It's difficult to maintain confidentiality in a small universe.
- Search is conducted and viewed differently in different parts of the world. Mature search markets have sophisticated methods to find and assess candidates, including passive candidates. In

developing markets, there can be constraints, including cultural and legal obstacles to approaching potential candidates. The process can be long and laborious, and expectations on both sides need to be clearly stated and realistically defined to avoid misunderstandings.

• Interviewers need to understand how to interview local and third-party nationals: what techniques to use, which questions to ask (and not ask), and how to interpret verbal and nonverbal signals of candidates from other cultures.

• Fluency in English should not be mistaken as an indicator of the overall quality of the candidate.

• The reputation of the local organization may not be consistent with the multinational's worldwide stature. Your search strategy should take into account the status of the industry, of the organization, and of foreign-owned companies in the country as well as the local employment situation.

• Some third-party nationals may not be comfortable in certain countries. Consultants need to be aware of historical, political, and cultural issues that may affect the conduct of the search.

• Overseas searches always take longer.

• Candidates may not be familiar with the executive search process. They may have surprising expectations. They may be suspicious or concerned for confidentiality. So they need careful attention and communication.

Bottom line:

• All parties must commit to make the extra effort needed to ensure mutual understanding and bridge cultural and communication differences.

• There must be agreement at the outset on clear and realistic expectations for the search.

• There must be continual communication among all parties, timely feedback, and clear explanations.

WHEN VIEWS COLLIDE: SEARCHERS AND HR EXECS

"Oh wad some power the giftie gie us, to see oursels as ithers see us!" This Robert Burns-ism seems especially appropriate for relationships between search consultants and their clients, including HR executives. It is truly a gift—when it happens—to be able to step into another's shoes.

As a closing thought to this section on working with executive search firms, it must be said that there always have been and are likely to continue to be differences in how the challenges of executive recruiting are viewed.

In many, many conversations over the years, we continue to hear that:

Search consultants believe they present qualified candidates in a timely manner almost every time. HR executives and line managers say not so much.

Corporate executives have a generally positive view of the hiring process at the executive level. They can see weaknesses in developing a clear need, scheduling interviews, and remaining committed to the project.

Search consultants say the corporate hiring process ranges from terrible to wonderful, usually driven by the strength of relationships between line managers, HR execs, and search consultants.

Despite the rise in influence of the HR executive in senior hiring decisions, search consultants are most devoted to CEOs and other senior line managers who drive decisions.

HR executives and line managers tend to view searches as a transaction driven by the immediate value of landing an excellent candidate. Search consultants, on the other hand, like to think that they can contribute much more value than a simple hire.

Corporate executives want search consultants to:

- Be honest earlier—honest about the candidate market, honest about what level of pay will be required to attract the candidates indicated, and honest about how long the search will take
- Communicate proactively—especially when things aren't going well
- Be realistic about their capacity to do the search well (do they have too many other commitments?)

Search consultants want corporate executives to:

- Be internal advocates for the search firm
- Move more quickly, with a greater sense of urgency
- Work around the process rather than be a victim of it (e.g., other interviewers)
- Sell the opportunity more vigorously

All worth considering!

4.

HOW TO ASSESS CANDIDATES
• • •

THE BASICS: COMPETENCIES AND INTERVIEW STRUCTURES

So much of executive recruiting is executing a checklist of procedures that consistently yield results and simply need to be followed diligently to achieve success. Then you get to the assessment of candidates: slippery, subjective, and prone to misjudgment.

Leadership development is one thing. There, you get to work with executives over time and see how they respond to a promotion, for example. But when you go outside at a senior level, stakes rise—and so do failure rates. If only we could predict executive behavior (actually, we have a piece on that later in this chapter).

Meanwhile, let's start with the basics. If you're using a search firm, by the time you're ready to consider candidates, you've had an in-depth discussion with the external search consultant on what you're looking for and it's clear that the consultant gets it. Further, the consultant has explored in detail—through phone and in-person interviews, and perhaps informal referencing—each candidate to be presented.

It would be good to know that every search consultant has a PhD in clinical psychology, but that's atypical. Search consultant skills skew toward sales, even though they may have developed keen skills in assessment in the course of their work. (Due to intense interest in assessment, search firms are quickly getting better at this.) On the hiring organization's side, a significant challenge is the fact that many hiring managers believe they are very good at interviewing, even though they have no formal training and sometimes limited experience at the executive level.

Behavior-Based Interviews

Overall, the most well-accepted tool for assessing candidates is the behavior-based interview. If you've ever had interview training, this is probably what you learned. It hinges on the idea that past behavior is the best predictor of future behavior, and that if we can gather credible examples of how the candidate performed in certain situations, we can develop reasonable expectations going forward. A behavior-based interview includes questions that begin, "Tell me about a time when …"

Competencies

Behavior-based interview questions are aimed at competencies, and here's where your leadership development partners can play a key role. They, perhaps together with you, should have established and updated evaluations of what competencies are successful in your organization and in the function in which the new executive will be placed. This becomes the foundation of the candidate assessment process. At its most basic level, these competencies should reflect an understanding of what capabilities are necessary at each executive level.

● ● ●

"We use structured assessments not just for selection, but also to inform reference-checking and the onboarding process." —STEPHANIE WARNER, CHIEF PEOPLE OFFICER, CONTINENTAL GRAIN CO.

Structured interviews

With relevant competencies in hand, interview questions can be developed, and interviewers can then each be assigned to address certain questions. The point is to cover everything without asking the candidate to answer the same questions over and over. It's a simple way to demonstrate to candidates that the hiring organization knows what it's doing. We are, after all, recruiting.

"We achieved more efficiency in the interviewing process by implementing pre-interview alignment meetings with the interviewing panel," says Dustin Fillion, Director, Executive Recruitment at Discover. "We discuss the position's desired mission, outcomes, and competencies so that all interviewers understand what they should be looking for in the right candidate."

WHAT TO ADDRESS IN CANDIDATE INTERVIEWS

David Kinkead, Kinkead Partners, based in Glastonbury, Connecticut, recruits commercial leadership for industrial manufacturers. He has 10 useful suggestions:

Read the resume beforehand. What strikes you? What isn't there that you want to know about? Are results quantified, and does it show clearly the difference this individual made to the organization? How well is it written?

Set the stage. Interviewing at its best is no more than a candid conversation, with questions inserted to direct the discussion toward information you need. Encourage the candidate's questions and be prepared to discuss shortcomings of the organization and maybe even yourself, if you expect the same. You must make it okay for the candidate to be candid and to know there are no deal-killing answers. If you hear scripted responses, call time out, ask for straight information, and promise the same.

Be clear and specific on what you want to know. Don't finish the interview with any questions left unanswered.

Ask about the importance of work to the candidate. Why do they work? Is it passion, a paycheck, work ethic, necessary evil?

Find out who the candidate is off the job. While avoiding questions that could cross legal boundaries, listen for clues to the candidate's personal beliefs, hobbies, and priorities. What's important besides work? What are their thoughts on work/life/family balance? Where did they grow up, and what was their early life like? Spending time here may yield information you can't ask about directly, but which if volunteered can be useful in understanding the whole person.

Ask about management style. How do they get things done through other people? Be careful not to lead with suggestions; see what the candidate has to say. Look for evidence of collaboration and genuine caring for people, with directive style reserved for last resort. Ask how they lead, motivate, inspire, share vision.

Who are the key managers they have hired, and what are their backgrounds? Get specifics on companies, education, and track records. Would you have hired those people? Are they outstanding and the best available? There can be some big surprises here.

What doesn't the candidate do well? To get straight answers, you may have to explain that we all have strengths and weaknesses, and that strong managers know their weaknesses very well. Ask how they compensate for them.

How are the candidate's thought processes? Are responses crisp and complete? Are they perceptive? Do they ramble or get off on tangents? Answer different questions than the one you asked?

Is the candidate personable? Do you like them? Are they real? This is the "Genuine Test." Nobody likes pat answers, and nobody believes them. Strong candidates will give a straight answer and let the chips fall where they may. They want to be hired for who they are, not who they can convince you they are. Also, are they upbeat?

HOW TO ASSESS FOR LEADERSHIP

We're good at assessing executives for technical skills and perhaps even for "fit" to our organizations. This is essential. But it's not sufficient if an organization seeks to hire leaders. So says Michael Feiner, consultant, former professor at Columbia School of Business, ex-Chief People Officer at PepsiCo, and author of *The Feiner Points of Leadership.*

As Feiner sees it, management is about producing order, and leadership is about producing change. So, rather than looking for those who fit, we're looking for those who create "followership." Great leaders, he observes, never work alone. While we think of Michelangelo as the genius who painted the Sistine Chapel, he had the help of 13 brilliant artists of the day and hundreds of helpers. When we think of Walt Disney as the father of animation, we need to know that he never drew a frame but rather brought together the great animators of his time.

Leadership is like an iceberg, Feiner says, with most of its substance hidden below the surface. It's the things leaders do that we don't see that accounts for their success.

And much is misunderstood: It's not about heroism, though many leaders are courageous. It's not about a grand strategy, because strategy is harder to implement than design. It's not about charisma, because you don't have to fill up a room with your personality to build followership. It's not about inspiring oratory, which is rare. And it's not about technical skills, even though one must be competent.

What leadership is about, Feiner says, is managing relationships—configuring them and influencing them up, down, and across the organization. He has a set of laws of leadership, including the following five examples, along with questions you can ask candidates to understand their leadership qualities:

The Law of Personal Commitment. This is showing real concern for and commitment to the people you manage—commitment to their career success as well as your own. Ask candidates: What's your responsibility in terms of commitment to your people? How do you demonstrate commitment? What have you done to develop people who have worked for you?

The Law of Feedback. Feedback—the leader's most powerful tool—isn't about "Atta boy!" but rather discussing what's been helpful in meeting expectations and what hasn't. Ask candidates: When do you schedule feedback sessions? What results have you seen when giving feedback? What tricks have you learned about giving negative feedback?

The Law of Tough Love. Tough love is tough both to give and receive. Leaders often avoid it because they don't want to demotivate. But it can be the only chance you have to create a winning situation. Ask candidates: Do you have examples of tough love you've had to give? What's the most important negative feedback you've received?

The Law of Competency-Based Coaching. The lower the subordinate's experience and skill, the more coaching a leader must provide. Ask candidates: What's your view about the importance of training?

The Law of Values-Based Leadership. "Values are the oxygen of followership," Feiner says, so we must understand what role values have played in a candidate's career. Ask candidates: Can you describe a situation where your values were challenged and how you handled it?

USING EXTERNAL ASSESSMENT SERVICES

Especially in direct executive recruiting, and sometimes when using search firms, you may be looking for a deeper dive on a candidate's suitability from an independent third party. Recent survey results show this practice growing to a point where most large companies in our survey sample are doing this.

The largest search firms and many smaller ones now offer assessment as a line of service apart from, or along with, executive recruiting. Korn Ferry (kornferry.com) is a leading player in this sector, having acquired two assessment specialty firms—PDI and Hay Group—to build its practice. Hogan Assessments (hoganassessments.com) has a long history in this field and is mentioned next-most-often in our most recent annual survey.

It feels as if there has been an explosion in the number of tools and firms in this space in recent years, but here are others often named by our corporate respondents: DDI (ddiworld.com); Russell Reynolds (russellreynolds.com); Gartner/CEB (gartner.com); Caliper (calipercorp.com); Gallup (gallup.com); Spencer Stuart (spencerstuart.com); ghSmart (ghsmart.com); Heidrick & Struggles (heidrick.com); YSC Consulting (ysc.com).

Russ Allison (racleadership.com)—who has conducted management assessments at a leading assessment firm (PDI, now part of Korn Ferry) in a corporate setting, at HP, and now in his own boutique consulting firm—describes four types of external assessment providers:

- Large executive search firms that have built or acquired assessment capabilities and bring to the table brand recognition, capacity, global reach, and often relationships at the board and senior management level
- Stand-alone industrial/organizational psychology and testing firms such as DDI, SHL, and YSC
- Boutiques, such as ghSmart, which can offer a high customer orientation, flexibility, and practicality
- Individual consultants, who can offer even more intimacy and capacity for trust, but who may lack capacity and availability

In practice, Allison says, most assessments across the provider spectrum are likely to reach the same basic, valid, and reliable conclusions on any given candidate. The challenges come in whether target roles are well-defined, whether the assessments are seen as credible, whether they are implemented properly, and whether they are followed up in onboarding and development.

PREDICTING EXECUTIVE BEHAVIOR

Is behavior-based interviewing good enough at predicting executive behavior? Clinical psychologist Dr. Leslie Pratch (pratchco.com) thinks not. Instead, she offers a more advanced way to evaluate business leaders.

Pratch says measures of past performance conflate individual capability with situational factors. Too often, hiring decisions are made without disentangling an executive's success from that of the firm where they previously worked. We have to go deeper, she says. First, we need to determine the core integrity of the executive in the context of an assessment of their whole personality. Second is to evaluate the active coping of the executive under the widest possible range of conditions and challenges. Both of these can be addressed through a clinical assessment.

The genesis of this approach was research she led at the Booth School of Business at the University of Chicago. The school asked her to determine how to predict which high-achieving MBA students in an elite program for future business leaders would emerge as the most effective executives. She discovered that by assessing an individual's coping style, she had a more reliable predictor of leadership than most measures provided. It became the basis of her doctoral dissertation, after which she earned an MBA and now consults to boards and private-equity investors, assessing individuals being considered for key management roles.

Assumptions

Pratch's work rests on four assumptions about personality:
• Personality is a theoretical construct that we use to explain how we think, feel, and act. We characterize personality in shorthand: Pat is self-confident and aggressive; Helen is empathic and intuitive. But such characterizations touch only a few of many parts in the makeup of whole personality—a rich and complex entity that can be rigorously and scientifically assessed.
• The effects of personality on decision-making can be predicted. With psychotherapy, certain aspects of personality can be changed.
• Our personalities are a function of our individual histories, especially our childhoods. This limits the extent to which we can change. Who we will be in the future is a function of the person we are today and who we were in the past. But some changes can be made with the right effort.
• Our personalities operate at different levels of conscious awareness. Each level affects how we think, feel, and act in ways that may not be obvious or easily measured.

In explaining personality, Pratch, like Feiner, uses the iceberg metaphor. Above the surface is what's conscious; below is unconscious; in between is preconscious, where we play with ideas coming to the surface (think of the fantasies of Walter Mitty). Much behavior is driven by what's below the surface, while at the conscious level, we believe we have control.

Sometimes we discover we don't have control when we do surprising things for reasons we don't understand and which may be against our best interests. We have deeper motives: hidden fears and wishes. The more aware we become of the unconscious dimensions of our personality, the more likely we are to be able to master them. Mastery becomes behavior that is flexible and strong—the hallmark of active coping. The better we cope, the greater our chances of being successful, Pratch says.

To *cope* commonly means to deal with or contend with difficulties. *Active coping* is the readiness to adapt resourcefully and effectively to complexity and change. We display it when striving to achieve personal aims and overcome difficulties rather than passively retreating or being overwhelmed. Active coping is a stable, albeit complex, psychological orientation across time and circumstance. It comes into play in a specific situation, in the now. It is almost always the best way to respond to a situation that was not, or could not be, anticipated, Pratch says.

Active copers feed on experience; they incorporate what they've learned into their psychological systems, making them increasingly more capable of tolerating uncertainty and devising new strategies for adaptation and growth. This leads to greater effectiveness.

Passive coping, meanwhile, is reactive and avoidant; refusing to tolerate the full tension a situation imposes; reacting before facts are sufficiently understood. Passive coping is retreating from reality, tuning out information and resisting change. It's dealing with minor problems in order to avoid the anxiety of major problems.

A clinical assessment

Interviews, like all self-report methods, permit canned or rehearsed responses. The questions are obvious, transparent, and easily manipulated. Most executives know what to conceal and reveal about themselves, their experiences, and the depth of their commitment. We call this "faking good." We may claim to be persistent and hardworking when what we really are is stubborn, Pratch says.

A way around this is to use projective techniques, asking candidates to supply words to finish a sentence or tell stories to describe pictures. Projective techniques represent vague, ambiguous stimuli. With little structure to guide the response, the candidate reveals more about underlying dimensions of personality. Pratch asks us to consider how we would complete this sentence: "When he failed in his work ..." Completing this "stem" requires the person to mobilize energy, orient attention and commit to making a response. If the person does not complete the stem, they have demonstrated passive coping.

Airplane pilots are tested in simulators that force them to cope with the unexpected. Projective techniques can work like a flight simulator to mimic stresses an executive would encounter. Executives who demonstrate active coping in structured situations may not be active copers at levels assessed by projective techniques. When measures on different levels disagree, a red flag goes up. An executive may present as an active coper but projective measures reveal he is anything but.

And guess what? Bottom line, under stress, this discrepancy will resolve itself in the direction of the underlying passive tendencies, compromising decision-making in real life. Pratch says she has found this to be true time after time.

What this means is that desires, fears, and conflicts beyond conscious control nevertheless drive and shape workplace functioning. Under stress, when our defenses may weaken, these warded-off parts of self are prone to appear. Familiar signs of passive coping include dithering, retreating into minutiae, paralysis, uncharacteristic outbursts of rage, and over-control of subordinates.

A real-life example

Mark was CEO of a Fortune 500 industrial firm. In less than a decade, he had led the organization from $83 million in revenues to roughly $3 billion. But recently the organization had come to a crossroads. Either it quickly doubled its revenues or it made itself an attractive target to be acquired. It also needed a new CEO, as Mark had announced he wanted to retire.

For two years, there had been no progress on either matter. The board of directors, concerned by the lack of a strategy and not seeing any capable successors, asked Pratch to assess Mark. Why was he not doing what had to be done?

Mark presented himself as—and was seen as—a big-picture thinker, charismatic, ready to change the world. He was also seen as hands-on, detail-oriented, hardworking, independent, and deeply knowledgeable about the organization's operations and products. Customers loved him.

Mark did have a few quirks. He refused to publish an organization chart and didn't give managers titles. Without clear lines of authority, they debated issues in seemingly endless meetings, after which Mark might arbitrarily overrule them. As a result, all important matters and far too many trivial ones were kicked upstairs to Mark. Consequently, the organization lost its most capable senior managers, and Mark's condescending attitude toward prospective CEOs alienated suitable outside candidates.

Here's where it gets interesting. By driving away capable executives, Mark, who tended to grandiosity anyway, became even more justified in seeing himself as the only person who could lead the organization—just as he alone had built it. It's true: He was adept at leading the organization when it was smaller and still ran it as if it were a startup. He wouldn't take advice or delegate authority.

Projective measures revealed that Mark was unable to admit he wanted power. Desiring power meant yielding to impulses that frightened him. The only way he could deal with anxieties these impulses trigger was to deny that power and authority exist. Because he feared power, he also feared that executives who have it would use it against him. So he did unto others before they could do unto him.

Mark's defensive structure had crippling consequences for his leadership. The organization's growth stressed his ability to control every aspect of its operations. When he needed to delegate and defer, he refused. He was coping passively by not adapting to the evolving demands of his role. Instead, he retreated into minutiae and dithered over matters his directors were begging him to resolve.

Under enormous psychological stress, Mark's coping was breaking down. Pratch's assessment clarified this dynamic for his board—and the board, finally grasping Mark's paralysis, took charge of recruiting a successor.

QUANTIFYING CANDIDATES: AN EVALUATION SCORECARD

So many candidates, so little time to really measure them. Faced with a handful of semifinalists for a key senior position and a several-member hiring team, we often try to make sense of it all by creating an informal scorecard with which to capture the evaluations of each candidate.

Weight the opinions of each member of the hiring team

In addition to deciding who's going to interview candidates, we need to think about how important a role each interviewer will have in making the hiring decision.

The vote of the hiring manager should probably carry more weight than that of the HR exec, for example. So, using a total of 100%, assign a percentage of the overall vote on each criterion to each interviewer. In one example, the hiring manager's evaluation was weighted at 50%; the recruiting manager's evaluation at 20%, a peer from another unit's evaluation at 20%, and a direct report's evaluation at 10%.

Weight the assessment criteria

Next is determining evaluation criteria. Say there are five criteria: leadership skills, management skills, relevant experience, a projected fit with the corporate culture, and an X factor.

Since the criteria are not of equal importance, they too are weighted: Let's say 30% for leadership skills, 25% for management skills, 25% for relevant experience, 15% for cultural fit, and 5% for the X factor.

Do the interviews and do the math

For each candidate, there's a scorecard. On the vertical axis are the interviewers; on the horizontal axis are the five criteria. Each interviewer assigns a numeric score to the candidate on each criterion, using a 5-point scale. There's room for comments along with each score.

Let's say the first interviewer rates the first candidate a 3 on leadership, 4 on management, 4 on experience, 3 on culture fit, and 5 on the X factor. Multiply each score by the criterion percentage weight: 3 times .30 on the first point; 4 times .25 on the second point, etc. Add these for a total candidate score for this interviewer.

Option: Give each evaluation a letter score

After calculating scores, you may find it handy to assign letter grades, to make the totals easier to look at for comparison. Regardless of how many criteria you use, as long as their weighting adds up to 100%, the following scale will work: 4.7–5.0 = A+; 4.3–4.7 = A; 4.0–4.3 = A–; 3.7–4.0 = B+; 3.3–3.7 = B; 3.0–3.3 = B–; etc.

Compare and discuss results

On a master scorecard, on the vertical axis, list all candidates and, next to each candidate, all interviewers. On the horizontal axis, list the criteria, followed by total score for each interviewer, alphabetical score and overall score. Take the total score for each interviewer, multiply it by the weight of the interviewer, and add them up for an overall score for each candidate. Discuss scores and comments, and proceed to the finals, for which you may want to end the scorekeeping and make final decisions based on additional factors and comparisons.

EMPLOYMENT REFERENCING: GETTING IT RIGHT

Candidate misrepresentation continues to be an issue. Studies show that 30%–40% of executives include inaccurate information on their resumes. Lee Pomeroy, a former search consultant at Egon Zehnder International, runs Executive References LLC in New York (executivereferences.com). He offers observations and advice:

- Reference-checking verifies claims made by the candidate in the resume (education, employment) or in interviews ("I was fully responsible for …") and it uncovers any potential problems, either personal or in the match of skills to the job.
- Information from references on candidate competencies can become a valuable part of a leadership development preview if the candidate is hired.
- The Fair Credit Reporting Act and other rulings might give employees access to reference reports about themselves, but there is no case law yet to shed more light on this privilege. Meanwhile, handle written references carefully. Use a summary approach, without individual attribution.
- There is nothing legally actionable in the verification of claims and matching of competencies.
- Conduct credit checks separately from reference checks.
- Be sure candidates know about referencing. Have them sign a release by the second interview.
- Permission to speak to specific references implies permission to speak to any references except those specifically cited by the candidate as out-of-bounds. Call more names than they give you.
- If references are told they'll be called, call them. Failure to do so is a disservice to the candidate (your new executive!).
- Make sure hiring managers aren't making premature reference calls (before candidate sign-off).
- When talking to references, avoid making candidates appear to be "applicants" for the job.
- If references refuse to provide adequate information, go to the candidate for help.
- Talk about reference-checking with your search consultants. Find out what they're doing and insist that they hit a high standard in this easily shortchanged area.

• How many references should be checked? "As many as it takes to hear a consistent story."

• When consulting your attorney, remember that lawyers take a least-common-denominator approach, which may not address the special situations of executive hiring.

What to ask

Some favorite reference questions:

• What areas would you recommend for development? or, If we were to build a development plan for this candidate, what should we include specifically for them?

• What was the candidate's greatest contribution/impact/legacy?

• What did you hire the candidate for and how was it accomplished?

• Would you hire this candidate again?

• What advice would you give this person's new boss on managing the candidate?

• How would you rank this person with others who have worked for you in the past?

• Can you give me an example of how this person demonstrated … ?

• In what areas did you provide the candidate with guidance and help?

• What's the one thing you would change about this person?

• How can we assure this person will be successful?

• Is there anything you'd like to add that I haven't asked you about? or, Is there anything that I should know that I haven't specifically asked you about?

• Who else should we talk to?

BASICS OF BETTER REFERENCE-CHECKING

"Everyone" knows how to conduct a reference check. But some things are so important it doesn't hurt to review basics. Search consultant Mike Travis (travisandco.com) makes the following suggestions:

• Establish rapport, make it conversational; the reference will be more open.

• Dictate the pace and take as much time as you need; if they run out of time, call back.

• Ask open-ended questions and listen carefully.

- Go beyond work history and seek insights into capabilities.
- Give recent references more weight than older ones.

What to cover

☑ Work relationship

☑ Impressions

☑ Interpersonal skills

☑ Communication skills (verbal, listening, written, presentations)

☑ Strengths

☑ Concerns

☑ Leadership style

☑ Motivation

☑ Ability to motivate others

☑ Work habits

☑ Planning skills

☑ Decision-making skills

☑ Adaptability, flexibility, pressure, and stress

☑ Ability to accept criticism

☑ Would you rehire?

NEW REFERENCING TECHNIQUES/TECHNOLOGIES

As part of today's heightened awareness of privacy and potential litigation, some corporate attorneys are advising HR teams not to conduct any candidate references, formal or informal. We might find this happening more and more as data privacy laws come to mean that all candidate records, including references, must be shared with candidates.

A few service providers are coming to the fore claiming they can circumnavigate this challenge. Checkster and SkillSurvey, for example, are advancing a model in which the corporate client asks the candidate to enter a number of references, by type. The request might be, for example, for peer, subordinate, and manager references from their last two employers. The systems then reach out to these references, ostensibly on behalf of the candidate, asking the questions the corporate client wants asked. The output is confidential and anonymized and is claimed to be a more effective tool than just "old school" referencing on its own. Perhaps this is the way forward …

WHO'S CHECKING BACKGROUNDS, AND WHAT ARE THEY SEEKING?

Important as they are, background checks on executive-level finalists are typically carried out by third parties. We queried 62 organizations on which agencies they use for background checks at the executive level. Among those, 82% use third parties and the great majority of those named a single provider.

And what are these agencies checking?

Virtually all check criminal records, education credentials, and employment records. About half conduct credit checks and drug screens. Smaller numbers of organizations obtain information on motor vehicle records, social media activity, professional certifications, civil litigation, fingerprints, and military records. A few use background checks for references, presumably beyond what has been done by in-house recruiters and/or search firms.

The most-often-named agencies conducting background checks for the surveyed organizations were HireRight (hireright.com), First Advantage (fadv.com), and Sterling (sterlingcheck.com). Also named by multiple respondents: Mintz Global Screening (mintzglobalscreening.com), Accurate (accurate.com), BIG (bigreport.com), and Pre-Check (precheck.com).

Eleven other agencies were named once each: A-Check Global (acheckglobal.com), ADP (adp.com), Career Builder (hiring.careerbuilder.com), Checkster (checkster.com), Cisive (cisive.com), Infomart (infomart-usa.com), KlinkCheck (klinkcheck.com), National Background Investigations Bureau (for government agency hiring; nbib.opm.gov), Orange Tree (orangetreescreening.com), Truescreen (truescreen.com), and Yale Associates (yaleassociates.com).

HOW TO HANDLE SOCIAL MEDIA BACKGROUND SCREENING

As recently as 2006, only about one in 10 employers used social media to screen candidates. Today, it's de rigueur. A 2018 Career Builder survey found 72% of employers screening candidates' social media presence.

Many companies do social media screening themselves, but some use social media background check consultants such as Social Intelligence (socialintel.com) for two main reasons: the cost of doing it in-house, where hours can be spent "going down rabbit holes" looking for inappropriate behavior; and the problem of finding something protected or sensitive that can't be considered when making hiring decisions but which can't be "unseen." Social media background check consultants typically provide reports on business-related online behavior only.

And sure enough, according to Social Intelligence, about 10% of these screenings turn up evidence of at least one of the following types of behavior:

- Demonstrations of racism/intolerance
- Potentially illegal activity
- Potentially violent conduct
- Sexually explicit material

In some industries, the hit rate for such behaviors is as high as 25% to 30%, according to Bianca Lager at Social Intelligence. She reports that 68% of hits contain racist, sexist, or intolerant language; 50% have hits in more than one category; and 8% have hits in all four categories. Sites yielding the most hits include Facebook, Twitter, Instagram, LinkedIn, Tumblr, Pinterest, YouTube, and Ask.fm.

Lager suggests the following best practices:

- Apply your Code of Conduct Policy or Social Media Policy to pre-hires.
- Decide who reviews reports—is it the hiring manager, HR, a committee?
- Consider a chance for candidates to correct content, for example, if a candidate has one or two flagged items, ask them to remove the content.
- Be consistent: screen all applicants or employees using the same criteria.
- Consider annual employee screenings.

5.

MANAGING CLIENTS AND CANDIDATES
● ● ●

In *The Trusted Advisor*, David Maister, Charles Green, and Robert Galford show the correlation between the depth of the consultant-client relationship and the breadth of business issues that any advisor (in-house or external) might be involved with. An advisor can grow from being a subject-matter (or process) expert to a consultant with a trust-based relationship, the authors posit. We have taken this model and adapted it to our world (see figure below).

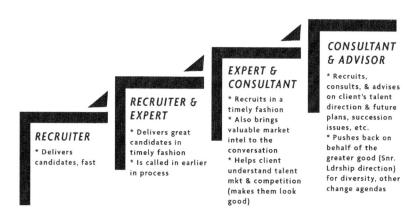

CONSULTANT & ADVISOR
* Recruits, consults, & advises on client's talent direction & future plans, succession issues, etc.
* Pushes back on behalf of the greater good (Snr. Ldrship direction) for diversity, other change agendas

EXPERT & CONSULTANT
* Recruits in a timely fashion
* Also brings valuable market intel to the conversation
* Helps client understand talent mkt & competition (makes them look good)

RECRUITER & EXPERT
* Delivers great candidates in timely fashion
* Is called in earlier in process

RECRUITER
* Delivers candidates, fast

An advisor builds a trust "bank balance" by making small deposits along the way. This is achieved by staying focused, listening, and framing the challenge in business terms that are understandable to the client. At the end of the discussion, there's commitment to an agreed solution to whatever the hiring challenge might be.

The authors use a formula to help explain this, whereby trustworthiness is equal to a numerator comprising credibility, reliability, and intimacy over a denominator of self-orientation:

$$T = \frac{C+R+I}{S}$$

In recruiting terms, this is best described as an equation of knowing one's domain expertise (leadership recruiting) and delivering consistent results, ideally above expectations and before deadlines.

We take the word "intimacy" to mean the amount of information that is above and beyond the strict data needed to execute a search— perhaps sensitive information that would not normally be shared— that a leader might trust an advisor with. For instance, if one were in a conversation with the CFO about hiring a direct report, the CFO might also share that they are considering retiring in a few years, and that this new hire could become a potential successor. This information might not be shared in a more public setting.

The point of the denominator of self-orientation is that we, as advisors, should take ourselves and our egos out of the equation as much as possible. We are there to consult, advise, and execute, and our expert opinion should enable a search to be completed as effectively and efficiently as possible. We are in the room as experts in our field and should "own our space" as such.

Though there is no single book one can read, or lesson one can take, to build gravitas and attain the level of trusted advisor, we have heard of a few tips and tricks.

It used to be said that dressing a certain way was important to gain credibility, but after having personally had meetings with billionaire executives wearing shorts and T-shirts, it's clear that different corporate cultures have different norms, and there no longer seems to be a one-size fits all standard.

Perhaps more important is the way one speaks and the language one uses. We must be clear and concise in dealing with the very top of the organization. Also, we should apply our knowledge to create a solution but describe it *in our client's language*. Part of our role is to make the business, the leader, and the executive hire more successful, so understanding the business challenges and how our recruiting solution matches them, is important.

Another tip—one of several from *The Trusted Advisor Fieldbook* by Charles Green and Andrea Howe—is to not confuse your metrics with your mission. In our terms, it might be that we're monitoring time-to-fill metrics, and the longer the search, the more those metrics suffer. However, if it's part of the business mission to make sure we consider underrepresented groups in our executive searches, then it's likely the search will take longer, albeit for the greater good.

We've heard useful tactics to help grow these skills from a number of ESIX members. One has created a team book club to read and review business books together and as a group learn from both the book and the ensuing discussion. Another corporate executive search team has set aside time at monthly meetings for team members to share difficult senior client interactions/challenges, and for the rest of the group to learn from those experiences and offer suggestions.

HOW TO COMMUNICATE WITH THE C-SUITE

As an HR or recruiting leader, getting things done means selling initiatives to top management. And to do that, you must think like a senior executive—and speak like one. A helpful report from the Society for Human Resource Management (SHRM's *HR Magazine*, Summer 2019) gives guidance.

● ● ●

"Relationships and strong influencing skills are critical in this environment." —JACKIE MORGAN, DIRECTOR, GLOBAL EXECUTIVE TALENT ACQUISITION, EATON CORP.

First, you need to understand how the organization makes money—beyond knowing what the organization does. What are the organization's biggest costs? What's the market for its products or services? Who are the key customers and competitors? What kinds of employees are vital to success? Let's say you're working with the CFO. Here, it's all about "What does this mean for the bottom line?"

Expect to make your case concisely, with precision and data. Show the tangible value of what you propose.

Get familiar with financial terminology, including EBITDA (earnings before interest, taxes, depreciation, and amortization), FP&A (financial planning and analysis), and P&Ls (profit and loss statements that show revenues and expenses for specific time periods). As an example, if you're working with the General Counsel, know that this function is all about lowering risk and liability. Learn as much as you can about employment law, including WARN (the Worker Adjustment and Retraining Act). And instead of saying to the General Counsel "Here's a problem," perhaps try "Here's a concern, and how can we work to address it?" A newer C-suite role is that of Chief Transformation Officer. That title can mean many things, so a recruiter must understand: *What exactly is that role in this organization?*

In general, here are some dos and don'ts in working with the C-suite:

• Do ask their preferred ways and frequency of communicating. Be mindful of their time. Pay attention to their personalities (is this person all business or do they enjoy small talk to establish a bond?). Bring data to support your suggestions. Ask for feedback.

• Don't use jargon. Avoid blindsiding executives by proposing big ideas with no notice. Don't propose a half-baked plan. And don't pretend to understand an unfamiliar term or subject for fear of looking naïve.

• Above all, don't be intimidated. When you approach a senior executive with a well-researched proposal, you deserve their respect—and you will get it.

PRACTICAL APPLICATIONS: THE KICKOFF MEETING

To help manage clients, we all have access to two basic tools that even the best of us may not be using to their full advantage: the kickoff meeting and the job description.

The kickoff meeting is our chance to set the terms of the engagement and to get everyone on the same page. Before we even walk into this meeting, we should have an understanding of what similar work we have done for this business group (just as a search firm would do). We also need to review the hiring manager's experience in recruiting at the leadership level. Don't get caught assuming that the hiring manager already knows the search process well. Better to make sure at each step that the hiring manager is getting it (without causing offense).

It's also important to discuss who will be on the interview team, especially if the hiring manager wishes to include team members who will report to the new hire.

Understanding who will have the most influence on hiring decisions is key, as is the question of which interviews/interviewers are "need to have" versus "nice to have," necessary at all, or possibly even detrimental to the candidate experience. (For example, research at Google has found that—for them—four interviews is optimal and more than that is potentially detrimental.)

It might even be useful to build a "RACI" chart or something similar, so all parties are clear on responsibilities. A RACI model clarifies who is **R**esponsible for a decision or action, who is **A**ccountable for the decision, who should be **C**onsulted beforehand, and who can be **I**nformed afterward; there are variations on this model, but they all help to make sure everyone's on the same page. The group making the final decision should be small—ideally only the hiring manager, the recruiter, and the human resources business partner.

Before the kickoff meeting, and during the conversation, any business, culture, or reputation issues ought to be researched and explored. We're often dealing with a small pool of prospects at this level, and typically the market is aware of leader or team reputations. It's important to get these things on the table early, so we can strategize over how to address them with potential candidates. Not only does this increase the potential pool, but it also shows candidates that our hiring organization is self-aware and on the path to resolving any issues.

It might seem obvious, but it's key for us to ask for a "no-go" list of organizations that should not be approached, and for what reason. Sometimes, that reason is not obvious. Perhaps there's a company on the target list that is in a strategic partnership with our company. Or there could be sensitive M&A discussions. Maybe our CEO sits on the board of the company whose CMO is a potential candidate. This does not mean we have to stop conversations with that CMO. But we do have to warn our CEO that there might be some uncomfortable phone calls coming soon.

We have often found it useful to have a conversation around "the perfect poster-child candidate, all else being equal"—that is, taking compensation, location, level, and other assumptions out of the picture—and what makes them so. You might also ask, "Whom have you modeled this new role after?" The hiring manager may have internal or external prospects in mind, but until asked, might not share. If the relationship allows, you could even go through their online network together to see who they think might be interesting for the role. These discussions may yield a prospect or two, but more importantly they help the hiring manager crystallize what they are really looking for, and they help you calibrate what "good" looks like in your prospect list.

The subject of possible internal candidates should be raised at the kickoff meeting, regardless of whether your model includes a review of internal talent before going outside. We have heard many horror stories of research being bought, candidate outreach being started, search fees being paid, and external interviews under way before the hiring manager is suddenly reminded of a perfect internal candidate somewhere else in the organization.

Timing is also an important factor to clarify in this meeting. Unless hiring managers are experienced at senior-level recruiting, they may expect the process to resemble the hiring of a new administrative assistant—that you will show them resumes in 48 hours and that the new hire will start in two weeks or less! As much as we don't want to terrify them, we have enough data over 20-plus years to say that an average hire at this level takes three to four months. Meanwhile, if you have data from previous searches, it might be a good time to show that good interview process management and prompt feedback can hasten the search considerably.

Critically, it's important to leave this meeting with the *top five criteria*. Does this really mean exactly five criteria? No. Should it be more than a couple, and yet still a manageable number? Yes. This criteria list becomes the core of messaging to the interview team as well as to the candidate. It also becomes the list against which we quantify interview feedback and compare the final candidate set.

Equally essential is that we leave this kickoff meeting with an agreement for a regular update meeting; this should be weekly, or biweekly at minimum. It's important that we all stick with this framework even if nothing has changed in the search, as it is the kiss of death when the recruiting team starts losing communication with the hiring manager. In fact, our experience is that, if we are not in regular contact with the hiring manager, the search will take at least 50% longer.

TO SLA OR NOT TO SLA?

The service-level agreement (SLA) question comes up from time to time, as in, who uses them and should we have the client sign something?

We believe SLAs are an extremely valuable tool, but not as a contract to be signed. They help to guide a conversation, especially for a new recruiter. But signing a contract may not be necessary. All you really need is a common framework to summarize the discussion you had and then send to the hiring manager to make sure you are all on the same page, especially with rough timelines attached.

DEFINING THE TARGET LIST

There is some debate as to whether we should enter the kickoff meeting with researched names and biographies that we have unearthed based on what little we know of the search. Some say this can go awry if we have things wrong, and diminish the hiring manager's confidence in our understanding or capability. Whether or not to introduce this research depends on the strength of the recruiter's trusted-advisor skills. If it's clear that the research is for guidance and calibration only, to help define the prospect pool, and we're confident we can own that conversation, then it can be extremely helpful. In other circumstances, this might be better kept for a second meeting. Whenever we choose to have the conversation, it is again as much an exercise in calibrating the exact search parameters for the recruiter and zeroing in on what the hiring manager is truly seeking.

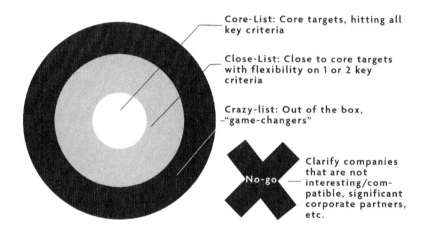

Core-List: Core targets, hitting all key criteria

Close-List: Close to core targets with flexibility on 1 or 2 key criteria

Crazy-list: Out of the box, –"game-changers"

No-go

Clarify companies that are not interesting/compatible, significant corporate partners, etc.

It's often helpful to categorize the research and biographies into three lists and guide the hiring manager through them. The first, or "core," list likely includes all of the usual suspects. If this is a particularly short list, it could help start the conversation about how restrictive the hiring manager's criteria are. The second, or "close," list might include prospects who do not meet all the criteria or who may have comparable alternative skills and experiences. This can help drive the conversation toward the option of a broader target candidate pool or, better yet, a more diverse one. The "crazy list" will test the boundaries of the search and show creativity, potentially opening the hiring manager's eyes even further. If we include people on this list who we believe are not even remotely likely to be hired, we can explore that unlikelihood and its reasons with the hiring manager. It's an opportunity to test assumptions, such as: "People from company X would never answer our calls," which could be because we have gotten used to not calling them!

In the same conversation, we might talk about "no-go" organizations, as mentioned earlier, but here it can be an opportunity to push back if the reasons are nonspecific or arbitrary. For example: "I used to work with someone from company XYZ, and they were terrible, so don't bring me anyone from that company." It's worth testing whether this is actually about the culture of that organization, or just an interaction with one person, as your prospect pool can rise and fall dramatically based on this determination.

PRACTICAL APPLICATIONS: THE JOB DESCRIPTION

Even the best of us are guilty of forsaking and abusing a basic tool of the trade—the job description—seeing it as a process step of little value. In fact, it is one of the most valuable steps in the search—the job description (JD) is in effect our contract with the hiring manager, as well as the hired candidate.

If we use the JD as a definition of parameters, then time spent clarifying it raises the hiring manager's engagement and, in our experience, shortens the search. It also aligns internal stakeholders, and particularly the interview team.

The JD should focus not only on the top five criteria, which would then be clear to any potential candidate, but should also dedicate space to specific outcomes expected of the role in the coming year. As an example, we can borrow a few bullets from our position spec for a Senior Corporate Executive Recruiter (see the Tools section in Chapter 7):

Responsibilities
• Conduct searches for the most senior positions in the organization
• Create comprehensive position specifications that support the definition, desired outcomes, critical qualifications, career-pathing, marketing, attraction, and selection of senior-level positions

- Source candidates through referrals, networking, social media, and search research
- Conduct detailed behavior-based interviews with internal and external candidates, providing information on professional background, career progression, alignment to role and organization, compensation, employment restrictions, regulatory licensing, and other required credentials
- Provide consultative advice across all aspects of executive recruiting (intake, attraction strategy, assessment, outcome management, offer, and pre-hire) while establishing trusted relationships

Related outcomes

- Meet the organization's hiring needs against specific metrics including days to fill, search firm utilization versus direct search, ethnic and gender diversity, offer acceptance ratio, and engagement completion rates
- Gain positive feedback from HR colleagues and clients, with consideration of overall corporate goals

COMMUNICATION, COMMUNICATION, COMMUNICATION

Though candidate volume and activity do not necessarily mean success, something should be happening every week, and keeping to the regular communication schedule is vital. "Client perception is reality," says Bertrand Dussert, VP Talent Acquisition at Tenet Healthcare. "In the absence of frequent signs of life, many clients assume nothing is happening."

Some hiring managers value long candidate assessments, and others want a high-level brief, so we should find out early what's expected or set expectations of what we're prepared to deliver. Whatever happens, we should continue to use the top five criteria as the premise for candidate descriptions and to provide market intelligence as trusted advisors.

Feedback on candidates from the interview team is critical and, along with market intelligence, helps refocus the direction of the search through continuous communication and calibration. As we hear all too often, the number-one shortfall of hiring organizations, and recruiters in general, is a lack of feedback and communication.

At some point, you may find yourself wondering why your senior client isn't responding to requests for clarification. Haven't your well-crafted, detailed status updates been treated like highly valuable information? Perhaps, like many hiring managers, your client is traveling at least half the time, reading messages on the phone and getting only to line 10 before moving on. A good lesson here is to put your "asks" first and make critical points in very few bullets. As a true trusted advisor, less can be more, at least until you need to show your homework.

A side point, but an important one: Develop a close relationship with the person who manages the hiring manager's time. These executive assistants are essential for getting extra time on the calendar when needed, or figuring out when the hiring manager will next be in Chicago to meet a candidate. You can make the assistant's job easier, too, by keeping them aware of schedule changes that may be coming up.

HIRING TEAM MANAGEMENT

Once we have all the information from the initial hiring manager meetings, we have a lot of what we need. In certain corporate cultures, it's not a bad idea to have a similar—perhaps shorter—meeting with other members of the interview team and the hiring manager's HR business partner, even if they were in the kickoff meeting.

Depending on the organization and how HR business partners work with executive recruiting, we do often hear that partnering closely with the HR business partner is valuable for gaining further insight into the role and the team. They can sometimes influence the hiring manager to go in directions that might lengthen the search, but be for the greater good—such as making sure to target a fully diverse pool of prospects.

Since we are more often than not creating customized compensation packages at this level, we must involve our executive compensation partners from the outset. Keeping them abreast of what we learn in the marketplace can speed things along and is especially helpful when board approval is necessary to make an exceptional offer.

Other best practices for the interview team are:
• Pre-send the job description, with the hiring manager's comments, which carry impact.
• Define each interviewer's area of focus to ensure clarity and improve the candidate experience.

• Include diverse members on the interview team, while avoiding tokenism.

• Meet before interviews to clarify the above and make sure they all get it!

• Have one person escort each candidate to interviews, to enhance the candidate experience as well as our understanding of the person.

• Gather feedback "on the fly" from each interviewer during the day by scheduling a five-minute debrief session after each interview and/or using feedback collection software.

• Meet after interviews are complete to gather group feedback, making sure one voice does not become the group opinion without discussion.

• Coach the hiring manager that not all interviewers are equal— that, for example, having subordinates of the potential new hire on the team does not mean that their opinions are equally weighted.

CANDIDATE MANAGEMENT

It's no shock to anyone in recruiting today that the candidate experience is key. At the leadership level, it's paramount.

As noted in Chapter 2, a "white-glove" candidate experience should be the first focus for any new corporate executive recruiting function. Putting the candidate at the center derives a positive return on investment almost instantly.

Indeed, candidates at this level are significant influencers, to be treated as major customers. They are typically not applicants, nor even actively looking. Instead, we have targeted them as successful leaders. As seemingly obvious as this may be, we must continually remind our hiring teams that we are recruiting the candidate and that the days of "show me why we should hire you" are truly over. At the same time, we're in the business of screening talent and so need to build a give-and-take relationship, which is part of what separates a good executive recruiter from a resume-pusher.

The closer we get to preparing an offer, the more important it becomes to avoid surprises. Expectations should be set, not only about compensation but about what else motivates the candidate.

The next step is big: Preview the offer with the candidate, so that any challenges can be addressed before a formal offer is made. You really don't ever want an offer rejected.

Who makes the offer? It's a lively debate. Some say it shouldn't be the hiring manager, while others see no need to protect the hiring manager and candidate from having a challenging exchange, since they will be working together for years (we hope!).

ONBOARDING

We all know that onboarding is critical—though unfortunately under-resourced—and that well-supported hires outperform and outstay others. And we've seen a gradual increase in onboarding programs in recent years. An advanced program uses data gathered during interviews, referencing, and assessment to develop and customize an onboarding and development plan for the new hire. To state the obvious: Ignoring this opportunity negates a lot of good work up to this point, and replacing a failed candidate—which is really a failed onboarding—is very, very expensive.

THE RECRUITER'S BIZARRE LIFE TRIANGLE (BLT)

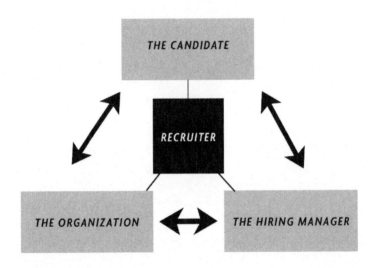

We executive recruiters exist in what you might call a Bizarre Life Triangle (BLT, hold the mayo).

It makes our role interesting and at times frustrating, yet we keep coming back because the subtleties and nuances, combined with the "super-secret-squirrel" nature of our work, make it so intoxicating. We get to change the fabric of the organizations we work for and help guide them to their aspiration states. And we do our work largely behind the scenes and unheralded. We are a strange breed living a strange life.

With apologies to everyone, especially to William Wordsworth and Shakespeare, consider the following ode:

> *I wander lonely as a cloud-based recruiter, never in the circle, always just on the outside—an observer;*
>
> *I love to watch people, to study them, learn about them, so much so that I became something of a square;*
>
> *Yet not completely, as I was always close to things ... no, not completely square;*
>
> *And at the same time, not in the circle, not owning the decisions, just party to them, advising them;*
>
> *Always watching, studying, questioning, learning, seeing;*
>
> *Yet more than just that—much more than that.*
>
> *Influencing, guiding, selecting, and sometimes, rejecting.*
>
> *In one corner,* **I protect my organization and its leadership, its protocols and policies***; though sometimes I break glass, not too much, and always for the greater good;*
>
> *Yet in the same instance, I support my* **hiring manager client***, and help move the business forward; I push for decisions, I drive for results, I deliver in a creative fashion.*
>
> *I am not afeard, I do not always jump whenever they shout, or ask "How high?" I follow the intent, not always the letter.*
>
> *But wait—in another corner I also advocate for* **my candidate***, ensuring their success and future, best positioning them to make the greatest impact on the organization, to change the world— while not giving away the farm;*
>
> *Aye, I am always between these three points—***organization, client, candidate;**
>
> *More mystical than a stuffy square;*
>
> *More points than a smooth circle;*
>
> *Always on the outside, yet always on the inside, working the three magical points together;*
>
> *Balancing the three, sometimes disparate, sometimes together, but always with me at the center:* **The Recruiter's Bizarre Life Triangle.**

6

DIRECT EXECUTIVE RECRUITING
● ● ●

THE BIG SHIFT IN-HOUSE

The use of in-house or direct executive recruiting in place of retained search firms has expanded—you might even say exploded—over the past 20 years. It's part of the larger trend toward corporate oversight of executive recruiting activity. Today, many large companies have a Director of Executive Recruiting coordinating the engagement of search firms to manage the process, avoid duplication of effort, and achieve better outcomes than the 40% failure rate that occurs when no one is watching. Companies that actively manage executive recruiting have cut failure rates in half, which is a big deal at a major organization.

> ● ● ●
>
> *"Hiring executives in my new organization felt that only executive search firms could find top talent. I was very surprised by this thinking and changed that view in six months."*
> —PAUL WARNER, DIRECTOR EXECUTIVE RECRUITING AND SYSTEM ONBOARDING, HENRY FORD HEALTH SYSTEM

The in-house model dates to the 1980s and originated in the banking industry, but more recently, technology companies and others across industries have moved most or in some cases all of their search work in-house. Our latest annual survey of 90 large organizations shows that 79% have an in-house executive search function. In-house executive recruiters typically have a retained or corporate search background with strength in executing searches (versus business development). A typical team includes four or five executive recruiters, each working on an average of eight or nine searches at a time, which is a somewhat higher workload than a consultant at a search firm might experience.

Conventional wisdom has been that in-house executive recruiters fill positions mainly in the US$200K–US$300K range, but today 88% of the in-house teams in our survey recruit for jobs above US$400K and 65% fill positions above US$900K.

Only a few companies attempt to conduct all search work directly. Most find it useful and necessary to use search firms selectively for the most difficult, unusual, or confidential searches. But direct-search advocates believe that in-house executive recruiters who really know their organizations can navigate through them more effectively and assess candidates for culture fit more accurately than external search consultants. An expert in-house recruiting function can also be given responsibility for internal mobility, applying the same skills to identify and evaluate internal candidates for executive roles.

"Building the asset of relationships with candidates over years pays back and is a reward for keeping a stable team," says Juan Calvo, Executive Search and Talent Movement Manager, Coca-Cola HBC.

PROS, CONS, AND GETTING THERE

Requirements
- Having "a product worth selling"; that is, an attractive organization (or willingness to try harder)
- Sufficient volume of executive-level searches (20 or more per year)
- Top management support that translates into influence with all hiring executives
- Someone running the practice who really knows the retained search process
- Dedication to research
- Time in which to build resources carefully and well
- Compensation of the search staff approaching that of search firms, at least for senior recruiters

Advantages (even if you're a wise buyer of external search)
- Search team's intimate knowledge of its organization and its industry

• No client blockages (off-limits) and just one client's interests at heart
• With no search firm to blame, the organization can focus on hiring effectiveness as an internal issue
• In-house team's experience makes the organization a smarter buyer of outside search services when necessary
• A strong in-house search practice capable of comparing internal to external candidates creates opportunities for better implementation of succession-planning initiatives
• Significant cost savings

Disadvantages

• In searches for functional positions, limited knowledge of other industries
• Lack of "marquee value" of outside search consultant and third-party "marriage broker" role that an external search consultant plays
• Possibility of angering competitors or corporate partners by making direct approaches

Challenges

• Educating management. There's a perception in using search that you turn on the spigot and get an immediate flow of candidates, when in reality what works is original research, which takes time. In the new paradigm, recruiters and researchers work on a modest number of searches at a time—not 25.
• Regulating the workload of the in-house search staff. Again, most companies don't have the volume to support the function; even those who do experience hiring lulls.
• Measuring hiring effectiveness well. This is key to understanding what works.
• Managing the sensitivity of raiding competitors—first by monitoring where candidates are coming from. A direct approach must be handled delicately (for example, always couched as a request for a referral or a networking connection). This includes a squeaky-clean approach to "rusing" (misrepresenting oneself and/or the purpose of the call).
• Setting clear limits for assignments the in-house search group will take (being able to say "no").
• Building the kind of research "reach" possessed by external search firms.

Overall success factors

- Associate the in-house executive search group with succession-planning efforts.
- Be patient implementing an in-house executive search function.
- Continue to "massage" the function; keep tweaking its structure and methodology.
- Keep communication active between in-house search professionals and top management (this can assist in "preventive retention" as well as recruiting).
- Hire in-house search team leaders who have an executive search as well as corporate background.
- Measure results: Track competencies, "stick rate," time-to-fill, costs, and diversity.
- Stay abreast of competitors' actions. Make it your business to know what works in other companies.
- Assist in onboarding. The in-house recruiting team is even better qualified than an external search consultant to anticipate and address issues that will help smooth the assimilation of new executives.

All told, says Joerg Ziegler, SVP, Global Head of Executive Search at NBCUniversal, "It's about managing the constant need for perspective on the marketplace and the talent within. We work very closely with our senior leaders and they lean on us for insight and guidance constantly."

FURTHER FINDINGS

Jones-Parker and Associates, a search firm specializing in recruiting search consultants for search firms and corporations, surveyed more than 150 HR executives in primarily Fortune 500 companies. Key findings:

Top reasons for building an in-house search capability were cost reduction (39%), faster searches (24%), more familiarity with the culture (24%), and more control over the hiring process (10%). Top benefits included reduced external fees (100%), better selection of external resources when needed (45%), more control over the process (27%), and a better understanding of the recruiting process (28%).

An in-house search capability seems to work best for large corporations, small fast-growing companies with big hiring needs, and private equity and venture capital firms seeking talent for portfolio companies.

Companies were recruiting experienced search consultants to help lead such efforts. This was seen as the desired profile by 57% of those queried; an additional 22% cited a contingency recruiting background (only 18% said a corporate HR background was desirable). HR executives still saw several advantages to using external search consultants judiciously: access to a broader talent pool (93%); able to attract better athletes (71%); can carry higher workloads (64%); and can better maintain confidentiality (50%).

It was suggested that to recruit search consultants or those with a combined search/corporate background, a compensation plan with wealth-building opportunities was needed.

Observations

Pay the group leader a base salary and a quarterly bonus based on the group's performance. For the group, take total revenue (in a chargeback model), back out costs, put 50% in a bonus pool, and pay quarterly bonuses to those who "sold" and those who "executed" searches.

In-house recruiters understand the culture better than external consultants but can be hindered by politics. They also spend more time than external recruiters at the "intake" meetings that launch a search.

Changes in job specs may occur more often for in-house recruiters; external firms often charge a new fee when the specification is significantly changed.

In-house recruiters are under more pressure to produce results. External search consultants manage expectations and dodge bullets.

A key issue in developing an in-house capability is maintaining a steady flow of search work for the staff. Some have considered serving outside companies on a selective basis, but the idea has not been embraced.

In-house recruiters sometimes find themselves competing in shootouts with external consultants. Dual searches have resulted (to cover off-limits).

Keep it simple: Start modestly by hiring a senior search consultant to lead an in-house effort. Begin by contracting for candidate ID and development with independent research firms until in-house search volume warrants additions to permanent staff.

BENEFITS OF AN IN-HOUSE SEARCH MODEL

In-house search teams have a stake in and knowledge of the

organization and knowledge of its culture and aims that cannot be duplicated by external recruiters. Their consistent relationships and the ability to know first-hand the organization's business needs and cultural fit are major benefits in identifying the ideal candidate success-of-hire and retention efforts.

The ability to leverage resources across divisions can be used to drive organization-wide initiatives such as increased internal mobility and workforce diversity. In-house search teams can proactively connect with a diverse community and introduce diverse executives in advance of an open position (e.g., diverse networking events customized to support underrepresented group gap analysis).

In-house recruiters can also be much more efficient than working with external consultants. The ability to leverage broad external talent pools for similar searches across divisions not only saves time and money by not duplicating search activities, but also makes for a better and more coordinated candidate experience. Further, it reduces expenses within divisions by avoiding search fees (a C-level search can cost US$750K–US$1M in search fees, even if an internal candidate is identified during the process).

Eventually, the in-house executive recruiting function's knowledge of the organization and talent, as well as the trust given by the business, starts to create a multiplier effect that is impossible to replicate with an external search firm.

Another advantage is the team's vested interest in hiring the best candidate for the job, since they belong to the organization and care about its overall success. Deep knowledge of the firm affords in-house teams the ability to support the organization's succession plans as well as provide external candidate identification where gaps are determined. And it has full access to all talent in the marketplace to find that candidate, including the internal candidate base—which is typically off-limits to outside search firms—as well as the ability to conduct confidential market intelligence in preparation for sensitive assignments.

Even if the in-house team is managing an external search firm on the project, the likelihood is that the search will close faster and with a much better result than if it is not properly managed by a dedicated function. And the ability to provide proactive recruitment strategies based on future business needs and known growth areas ultimately reduces time-to-fill.

In sum, having a dedicated team of in-house executive recruiting experts will not only save money on search firm fees, but also by making sure that the right level of expertise is dedicated to the work. Using inexperienced internal recruiters to save money, or paying cheaper external recruiting or contingency firms, can waste more money in the medium to long term, as they might result in lower-quality hires or insufficient due diligence.

COLLECTIVE WISDOM ON THE IN-HOUSE INITIATIVE

We ask heads of in-house search teams from time to time to state their success factors. Here are the points we hear being made again and again:

- Stay small, or at least start small.
- Make sure management backs you.
- Pick the right point of entry, where you know you can generate early wins.
- Start with functional roles: IT, finance, HR, legal, marketing.
- Align search team members by function and line of business.
- Hire some people with retained search experience.
- Coach executives on how to interview.
- Meet candidates first; if possible, travel to interview them before bringing them in to meet senior hiring managers.
- Insofar as possible, be faithful to the process of retained executive search.
- Because research is not done as easily from the inside (you can't make calls without naming the client, for example), consider buying some research externally.
- Keep executive recruiter workloads reasonable.
- Meanwhile, try mightily not to turn down searches for lack of capacity, though consider turning down searches that are most difficult or very rare.
- Learn to recognize situations in which an external firm is the better choice.

● ● ●

"Build buy-in at executive level, but don't rush it. Know where things stand. Don't push on doors that are closed. Build slowly: One great search executed well is much better than three or four done to a lower standard. Also: Focus on executing an effective process and a positive candidate experience. Your candidates soon become your internal clients and this is critical to building brand and a strong reputation within the organization." – JULIA MARKELL, HEAD OF EXECUTIVE TALENT ACQUISITION, MONDELEZ INTERNATIONAL

LESSONS LEARNED IN BUILDING AN IN-HOUSE FUNCTION

Bertrand Kimper, Head of Human Capital Strategy & Planning at Johnson & Johnson, offers the following advice in establishing and growing an in-house executive search function:

It's not about the money. If you are highlighting search firm cost avoidance to leadership, you may be challenged and asked if actually there should be a price tag on hiring top executive talent. Read your audience! While money is an issue for some, we learned to focus on the quality of talent placed, what they have contributed to the organization, and how this has created options for succession planning.

Add value beyond search. Broaden your offerings to include executive talent move tracking, mapping, pipelining, a diversity and inclusion initiative, and market intelligence. This diversity of services keeps us closer to the businesses.

Executive referrals are underrated. A good way to market an in-house function is to build a strong executive referral program, which gives you premium access to business leaders across the organization.

Not all executive recruiters are wired to succeed in-house. An executive recruiter can be very strong as an external consultant, but may lack the ability to navigate in a matrixed corporate environment and manage a complex internal hiring process. The most underrated skill in in-house recruitment is an agile mindset.

Don't take it personally; focus on the long term. We once pitched for a very senior role focused on innovation. The incumbent said he would never pick up the phone for an in-house executive recruiter and would answer calls only from well-known search firms. Two years later, he had moved on, and we backfilled his position and his peer's position through the in-house team. You have to be patient!

Demystify executive recruitment. The better you can educate your hiring managers on the relevant search firms and their strengths and weaknesses, the better you can make the case for the in-house function.

EXAMPLES OF A CHARGEBACK MODEL FOR IN-HOUSE SEARCH

Most companies in our annual Benchmark Survey have a capability to recruit directly at the executive level. Many conduct a significant portion of the search work directly, without search firms. In building budgets for these functions, thoughts often turn to a chargeback model to fund the cost of in-house executive recruiters. But few have successfully implemented a chargeback.

To be clear, a chargeback refers to attaching a fee to in-house search services and billing that fee to the hiring manager or business unit being served. Here are a few examples from the last few years:

At IBM, the in-house team charges a flat fee based on the level band of the position, with the fee ranging from US30K to US$60K, and an additional fee for subsequent hires from the same search. IBM's comment was: "We have been quite generous with the definition of a by-product hire for groups that have engaged with our team for multiple searches. To date, I have not had a client decide not to use our service due to the fee."

At Philips, the model was "straight fee for service," and a full executive search was billed out at €25K (US$32K). Project management of a process that included a talent scan beyond identified internal prospects cost €10K (US$13K). Search firms were engaged only by the in-house team, and there was no fee for managing a search being conducted by a search firm. Philips' commentary at the time was: "We will likely add a fee as we develop a standard way of in-house managing/working with external search."

The Philips team also offered a pipeline/external succession planning service at €30K plus a full fee when a formal search was launched or when a talent pipeline candidate was hired. And for a competitive intelligence project, the team charged €8K or a fee based on the scope of the project.

At Coca-Cola, the chargeback fee was 15% of cash compensation (base plus target bonus), in three increments: 5% for the research; 5% for a completed slate; and 5% if an external candidate was hired.

Finally, at Warner Media Group, the chargeback was a fixed fee billed quarterly to each division and based on the size of the business unit and its headcount. The function leader at the time commented: "Over our lifecycle, we have gone from no chargebacks at all, to transactional chargebacks, to the current fixed chargeback model. We were not a fan of transactional (even heavily discounted at 5%, 7%, and 10%), as it encourages the same behavior many companies use with search firms—i.e., 'Let's try it ourselves, muck it up for a few months, and then use us as a last resort.' It also diluted one of the great values of an in-house model—being part of the dialogue very early."

You might think of the evolution of an in-house search function as a pyramid that mimics Maslow's Hierarchy of Needs, a model of personality development which posits that basic needs must be met before an individual can advance to the next level. In the following model, the first level includes the basic characteristics and achievements of the function. As credibility of the function rises, so does its participation in strategic initiatives, until reaching the pinnacle of involvement in anticipatory actions affecting top positions.

CORPORATE EXECUTIVE RECRUITING BY MASLOW

BOARD/CEO HIRING & SUCCESSION; TALENT/MARKET INFORMATION BEFORE DECISIONS ARE MADE

STRATEGIC CEO, SLT REPORTING; DEFINE CRITICAL TALENT GAPS (NOT ROLES); CREATE PIPELINES & SENIOR TALENT COMMUNITIES; INTEGRATION W/ SUCCESSION PLANNING/TALENT MANAGEMENT

EXCELLENT CLIENT SERVICE; CONFIDENTIALITY & TRUST; HIGH-TOUCH CANDIDATE EXPERIENCE; ACTIVITY REPORTING; COST AWARENESS

CREDIBILITY BANK BALANCE OVER TIME

ENVIRONMENTAL REQUIREMENTS FOR BUILDING AN IN-HOUSE TEAM

Once it's clear that you have sufficient executive search activity (20 or more per year) to warrant establishing an in-house team, then the most important factors are sponsorship and strategic investment in the long term. Everything else cascades from these:

• Creating such a model will take time, both to deliver quality product and to gain the credibility to influence at the highest level. It's a long-term, strategic function that depends on support for the model when budgets are tight.

• Similarly, support will be needed to help wean senior leaders away from their "pet" search firms—or at least to allow the in-house team to manage the relationship/offer an alternative, thus giving them time to build credibility.

• The best teams have a mix of ex-search firm members as well as top-tier corporate recruiters—neither come cheap, and there will need to be a recognition that an investment in team compensation will have to be made that may not pay off for at least two years.

• There should be absolute clarity that the team workload will be carefully managed. The highest-quality, most impactful work can be carried out at a workload of around 6–10 searches per client-managing executive recruiter at any one time, at different stages of work, and no more than 15 in a year (note that candidate-generation role numbers are likely to be higher).

• It should be patently clear where the lines are, and when the group is able to say "no"—especially as they become successful. Suddenly, they will be asked for "favors" to "just do this one search," even though it's below the team's remit.

• Sometimes "air cover" might be needed; for instance, when someone at a strategic corporate partner is approached as a potential candidate or when one of your executives is on the board of a target organization. Part of the value of such a team is that this should already be well known and contingency plans should already be in place for such situations.

• Finally—and critically—there should be regular and iterative communication on the activities of the group, interacting with the CEO and board if possible, and certainly at the Chief HR Officer level.

TEAM METRICS AND REPORTING

In most cases, recruiters are measured on standard criteria—for example, the number of closed searches/hires (not always the same thing if involved in internal talent movement); the number of projects, if recruiters are involved in talent-mapping or succession; time-to-fill; time to introduce final placement; diversity of pipelines, candidate slates, and hires; and so on. More-advanced models focus on other factors, such as the proportion of organization-critical or strategic hires compared with "regular" executive hires, placement retention, candidate/placement competencies compared to organization/internal norms, senior leadership feedback, and succession planning indices.

One notable risk in using senior leadership feedback as a metric is that recruiters will sometimes have to move a bigger rock than just making a hire, perhaps in ensuring a diverse candidate slate, which may make a search take longer than the hiring manager is comfortable with.

Some teams have moved away from individual recruiter metrics and goals to focus only on a team goal, with the view that each team member brings value to each interaction for the overall good of the organization.

The question of what metrics we ought to report to the C-suite comes up a lot, and our opinion is that whatever we report, it should not be about standard recruiting metrics. This may sound heretical, but the idea of measuring only our activities (time-to-fill, candidates per hire, etc.) is useful for us but not helpful to management, where the interest is in impact on the organization. For reports to top management, we suggest measuring strategic talent gaps, analyzing our competitors, and discovering and sharing competitive talent information with the head of HR and the CEO. We have access to all of this information, but often miss the opportunity to use it.

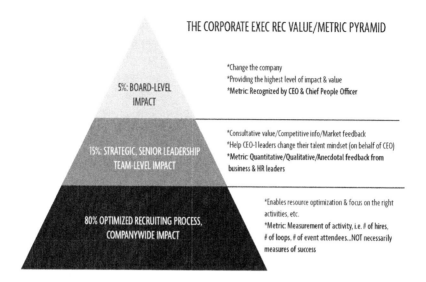

THE CORPORATE EXEC REC VALUE/METRIC PYRAMID

5%: BOARD-LEVEL IMPACT

*Change the company
*Providing the highest level of impact & value
*Metric: Recognized by CEO & Chief People Officer

15%: STRATEGIC, SENIOR LEADERSHIP TEAM-LEVEL IMPACT

*Consultative value/Competitive info/Market feedback
*Help CEO-1 leaders change their talent mindset (on behalf of CEO)
*Metric: Quantitative/Qualitative/Anecdotal feedback from business & HR leaders

80% OPTIMIZED RECRUITING PROCESS, COMPANYWIDE IMPACT

*Enables resource optimization & focus on the right activities, etc.
*Metric: Measurement of activity, i.e. # of hires, # of loops, # of event attendees...NOT necessarily measures of success

As we go up the "strategic value chain," we report less on our activities and processes while at the same time our work becomes more impactful and confidential. If we're planning for our CEO's succession, for instance, or hiring board members, then the only people likely to know about these activities are the CEO, the board, and the head of HR.

TACTICAL ADVANTAGES OF AN IN-HOUSE TEAM

In addition to strategic reasons for building an in-house team, there are tactical advantages:

• Executive recruiters who really know their organizations can navigate through them more effectively and assess candidates more accurately.

• A dedicated team can develop an incomparable knowledge of the industry and the competition.

• An expert in-house search function can also be given responsibility for internal mobility, applying the same skills to identify and evaluate internal candidates for executive roles.

• Issues of candidate blockages due to other customer relationships (i.e., off-limits) are virtually eliminated—you have only one customer!

• Responsibility is clear: If there are internal or cultural issues to be addressed, no one can blame the external search firm, and an internal model is more likely to surface such issues to the right people, for the good of the organization.

• There's opportunity to develop, grow, and continually adapt the function so it becomes part of the fabric of the organization and an asset to the senior leadership team, both in providing competitive advantage as well as assisting the CEO/board with change initiatives.

NOT FOR EVERY SEARCH

We don't expect an in-house search team to handle everything, although if a search firm is used, it should be managed by the in-house team.

For some corporate roles, searches happen infrequently—to a point that there's no strategic value in building market knowledge in those areas. This can be the case for positions that are filled only once in five years, for example, or for roles that are not mission-critical.

Over time, an in-house team develops an intimate knowledge of its normal searching territory. But if the organization is entering a new market space (product line or industry, perhaps through acquisition), then it may make sense to engage search firms until new in-house "search muscles" are built.

Sometimes there's value in using an external firm even if your in-house team is capable. Some prefer to use search firms for board searches, or even CFO searches, even if the in-house team still does most of the work, to ensure that shareholders feel that an unbiased perspective was sought.

Finally, for new internal clients, even though your team may have the expertise, some hiring managers will react more positively to the halo effect that an external search firm can bring, while the in-house team's credibility is still being established.

IDEAS ON A FUNCTIONAL MODEL

Having studied in-house search models at many large companies, we find strong similarities. Depending on resources and scale, the function is usually broken into four or five segments divided along these lines:

• Function management—about 20%
• Candidate experience, operations and logistics—about 25%

- Candidate research and possibly outreach—about 10%
- Client and search management—about 45%

One version of this model is outlined in the diagram below and includes an additional Community/Prospect Relationship team, which some organizations include in their Operations headcount. Also worth noting in the diagram is how the entire function organizational model pivots around the core of the function's mission, which might include something around hiring more diverse leaders, for example.

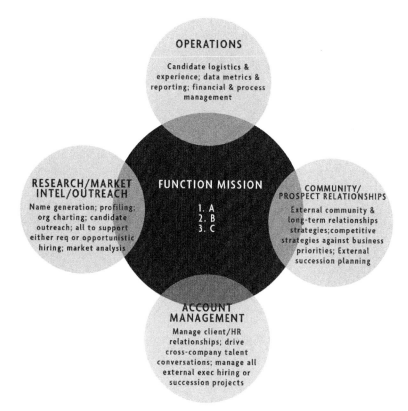

PIPELINING

Pipelining is best described as a methodology organizations can utilize to create a constantly refreshed pool of talent that the organization can then hire from at any time. The opposite would be connecting with the talent pool only when a requisition opens.

One of the simplest tools to help non-experts to understand why an organization should invest in strategic pipelining is the following Venn diagram:

...or just the best of those that apply?

To begin, most organizations proudly say that they are hiring the "best and brightest." But if they are operating on an applicant-based hiring model, then technically they are hiring only the best of those who apply. Since our focus is leadership recruiting, it is unlikely the reader will be planning an applicant-only recruiting model.

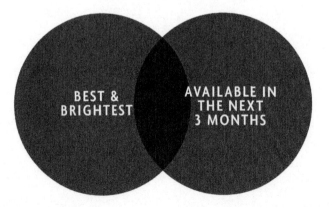

Next, we introduce a variable into the diagram, whereby we realize that most leadership roles open when the position is vacant or new, and then take an average of three to four months to fill. So, if we operate a requisition-based, on-demand hiring model, then we are always looking for talent that's available when the requisition opens. If our recruiters are diligent, research and outreach will continue even after a shortlist has been provided. This is unfortunately not the norm.

As we add yet another variable—relocation—it becomes obvious that we are really recruiting from a small subset of the overall best-and-brightest pool.

However, if we operate a strategic pipeline model, whereby we gain an understanding of the entire leadership talent pool, it helps us understand the lay of the land. If we add to that a knowledge of future succession or critical talent needs in our own organization, then we have the basis of a true pipeline model, whereby we can start to plan and develop talent relationships well ahead of business needs.

To take this a step further in a talent-centric culture, one can move to an "opportunistic hiring" model, whereby we come to know the talent and their motivations, and ideally hire when they are ready to move. Though we are still not looking at the entire best-and-brightest talent pool, we are at least able to work with a much more significant proportion of it.

**KNOW THE TALENT OVER TIME AND HIRE
THEM WHEN THEY'RE READY**

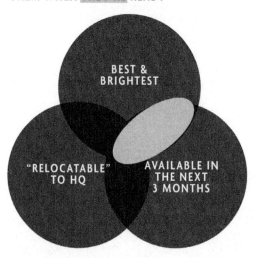

Of course, in an ideal world, we would have free access to all available talent, could hire them when their motivation is right, and have no friction around talent movement or relocation.

Meanwhile, there will always be a few "anti-company zealots" who will never be persuaded to join the organization. But by removing two of the largest obstacles to the free flow of talent, we are dramatically increasing our potential talent pool.

ANATOMY OF A PIPELINE

Variations on the model

Most recruiters—and salespeople and marketers—have seen and used the concept of the pipeline. There are a few variations on this tactic related to leadership hiring which merit explanation:

Critical talent/succession gaps. The first of these variations actually has nothing to do with the talent pool, but is all to do with the direction of the organization. Without understanding what the future leadership talent needs might be, the pipeline is a ship without a rudder. This might be as simple as knowing that the Chief Financial Officer plans to retire next year or, at a more strategic level, it might be an understanding of the 10-year plan for the organization and the corresponding leadership talent gaps and implications.

Research. There are numerous research tools available, which we hear about through our ESIX Research Roundtable, and the ability to access talent data seems to grow daily. The corporate leadership recruiting research function is really starting to take hold and we are excited to see the function develop and grow.

Internal calibrations. The premise here is that your organization's current employees ("sources") might have worked with or have opinions on leadership employees ("prospects") at your target organizations ("targets").

Keeping in mind any relevant non-compete or non-solicit clauses that might inhibit the sources, some leadership recruiters hold meetings with individual sources or sometimes small groups—perhaps all those who used to work at target company X at a senior level. The idea is to map the leadership at target companies, using either an in-house or external research resource, then use the maps to spur a conversation about prospects. We recommend maintaining a structure to that conversation, perhaps with a grading scheme ("definitely should explore," "needs more investigation," or "do not recommend exploring"). There should be evidence to support the opinion to avoid generalizations such as "would not fit" or "would not work with again." Such data should be time-referenced as much as possible. Sources sometimes "play old tapes" when meanwhile the prospect has actually learned and grown since they worked with your source.

This kind of "target mapping" has the added benefit of not putting the prospects at risk of industry gossip, nor does it disclose what roles your organization might be recruiting for.

Finally, it's important that all such feedback is "triangulated" with other reference points, just as we would do with normal references (see Chapter 4) to make sure we have all sides of the story.

Engagement strategy

Here we can begin to plan how we will engage our prospects, making the most of our resources, including leaders in own organization who are adept at developing external talent relationships ("evangelists"), perhaps who also have networks inside your targets. These resources might also include industry conferences that your prospects are known to attend or speak at. You can then discover which of your own organization's leaders might attend. Another resource might be prominent industry research institutions, or associations, where some of your own leaders may have networks.

Outreach

As we start to connect with prospects, the first approach may come from a leadership recruiter but may also come from talent evangelists described above—for coffee at a conference or a meet-up as industry peers "next time I'm in town."

"Executive Introductions, particularly of diverse talent, provide internal senior leaders with a pipeline of exceptional talent for opportunistic hiring," reports Judy Wong, VP Corporate and Executive

Recruiting at Charter Communications.

Networking Events

A seldom used but effective tactic at this point is the leadership networking event. This can take the form of an exclusive, highly curated invitation-only dinner where the invitation list is perhaps 25 people at most (10–12 participants from your high-value prospect list, 6–10 senior talent evangelists from your organization, and a few significant external players who may not be prospects but are potential talent "magnets"). It might be a special-topic dinner, with the magnets— experts such as academics or authors—joining a panel with one or two of your leaders. Invitations might come not from the recruiting team but from the senior evangelist.

The "secret sauce" to these events is part extensive planning (logistics, environment, speakers, invitation list) and part the way evangelists are managed and the output expected of them. Each should be briefed on a subset of prospects, including pictures, bios, and any calibration information.

Evangelists are tasked with going deeper into a certain topic with their prospects, gathering more information, and providing a report card with evidence to support their perspective. That recommendation should include who might make the next approach. At the end of the event—that very same evening—evangelists meet to discuss grades and evidence for their recommendations. At this point, the best-of-the-best list starts to form, along with your continued engagement strategy.

Cultivating relationships

As the relationship with the prospect grows, more motivation data is collated and over time, the right time to hire is discovered, and then the normal process of hire and offer is followed.

EXTERNAL SUCCESSION PLANNING

Although implicit throughout this chapter, it must be said explicitly that the success of pipelining programs is predicated on a talent-centric culture. These programs would be much more challenging to initiate and maintain where talent is seen as only a cost, or expendable, and recruiting is seen as a transaction, as opposed to a strategic tool.

It's also important that there is a culture of information sharing between leadership recruiting teams and management development teams, especially as it involves development and succession plans, as well as capability gaps in the current leadership. If these two organizations work together seamlessly, there is significant competitive advantage in being able to "see around the corners" when it comes to leadership talent. This is a critical process that we call External Succession Planning (ESP).

A successful ESP program depends on a few foundation principles:

• A proven pipeline process for internal talent must be in place, so that leaders are trained to think about this in a strategic way. They should also be coached on how to have conversations with prospects without a job description in front of them. It's surprising how difficult this can be for some senior leaders.

• There must be a regular, structured communication/reporting relationship with senior leadership, including the CEO as well as the CHRO.

• There should be clarity and agreement on critical talent gaps for the organization—not just open roles, but capability gaps.

• There should be integrity in the succession plan, not just an annual fill-in-the-blanks exercise with the same names every year, some appearing in numerous boxes across the organization. And when we include external prospects in the plan, these are not just names and bios of people no one has met; they are prospects on whom we have significant calibration and who have met and begun a relationship with the succession plan incumbent or their manager.

• You'll need a functioning CRM/search management software tool to hold information on prospects—remembering that these are not candidates and are therefore not in an applicant-tracking system—in a secure, relational database that can cross-reference multiple relationships and connections. If this system can talk to the succession planning system, all the better; but so far that's an unlikely scenario.

• And finally, to reiterate, it's key that the leadership recruiting team has a strong, trusting relationship with Talent Management, or whomever owns internal succession planning. Otherwise this model is not possible.

Getting started

Here are some hints on how to approach this methodology, which are unsurprisingly similar to those we would share before anyone decided to create an in-house executive recruiting function.

- The first of these is to **start small**, and perhaps even stay small if headcount and resources are a constraining factor. It's very easy to get wrapped up in trying to "boil the ocean" with a program such as this, and once success comes, everyone will want to share in it, which could create significant challenges if scaling is not possible.
- As always, **make sure you have the backing of senior management**, as this is a long-term strategy that may not bear fruit for at least a year, or at least not at scale, and will need sustained support through multiple budget cycles and regime changes.
- Again, just as with most innovative programs, **pick the right point of entry and generate early wins**. It's best if you can find a "poster child" leader/incumbent to work with first—someone aware of the challenges of the external talent market and, ideally, well connected externally and well respected internally.
- After a few wins with this leader, have them help with your "PR." It can also be helpful to generate some internal competition among other leaders who also want a piece of the action once they hear of your success.
- The right point of entry will likely also include highly critical roles—ideally, those peculiar to your industry. In other words, unless Human Resources or Accounting is critical to the growth of your organization, they are not likely places to launch this model. You need talent gaps that are "make or break" for your organization to make sure you have maximum attention from your leadership team.
- Finally, you'll need a direct reporting or communications channel to your senior sponsors, ideally the CEO and head of HR, so you can update them on progress and enlist their help to persuade or coach certain leaders as needed.

Critical Talent Gap Alignment and Reporting

A "critical talent gap" refers not to individual roles or requisitions but to talent types, or sets of skills and competencies, that the organization realizes it's lacking. This could be data analytics or "digital"; perhaps AI or strategic thinking; and, naturally, diversity of leadership. It's likely that this vacuum exists throughout all levels of the organization, which is why a critical talent gap audit carried out in partnership with the entire Talent Acquisition team might be most effective.

Here is a simple framework to at least get everyone moving in the same direction.

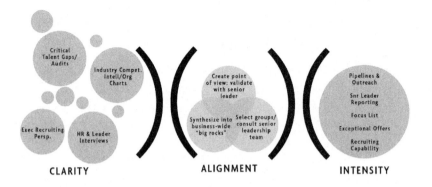

The first section of this model—gaining **Clarity**—is all about information gathering, as well as putting a line in the sand as to what the critical talent gaps are for your organization. Considering the level of work we do, and the access we have, it's likely that we already know exactly what these are ahead of time. But there's nothing like having data at hand to clarify issues for others and demonstrate the value of our function.

First, we ascertain the critical talent gaps for the entire organization and verify them with the CEO, the CHRO, and so on.

Next we gather all relevant competitive talent and market information to serve as a backdrop for interviews with senior HR function and business leaders. We ask each business leader and HR partner what their needs are in relation to critical talent gaps, now and in the future. This can include looking at succession plans and discussing the movement of internal talent.

With all of the information from all of the above, we can approach an **Alignment** meeting, where we review and synthesize data and evidence into key themes. Specifically, we're talking about a meeting where, with all leaders in the room, priorities are set on where to focus resources— i.e., on critical talent gaps—and which talent profiles might accordingly receive less attention. Of course, we often hear complaints a week after that meeting that the leaders' openings are not getting equal focus, specifically those we had agreed would receive less attention, even though we had commonly agreed on a priority list just a week before! This is one of those times that great meeting notes are helpful, as well as a recap email to all attendees on decisions made!

Getting business leaders on the same page as you and each other, and then holding them to that agreement, is an interesting part of our lives—part of the "Recruiter's Bizarre Life Triangle" (Chapter 5).

Once this part of the model is complete, we will have the agreement of business leaders and the overarching senior leader on what the critical talent gaps are, which business leaders will put more emphasis on them, and how and where to spend resources to address those challenges. Now we have our marching orders and can work on critical talent gaps with **Intensity**, including creating talent prospect pipelines and perhaps networking events, as outlined above.

We might increase our recruiting or research capability, and even start the process of having the head of executive compensation—and perhaps even the board, if necessary—preapprove exceptional offer ranges ready for the new critical talent we will be bringing on board. We also advocate specialist reporting to the senior leader specifically and separately on this program's progress, which might include the creation of a Top 100 focus list of prospects (or whatever number works for your team). This reporting could also include giving praise to business leaders who are going out of their way to increase the critical talent capability in your organization: If it is important to the business, then the senior leader (perhaps the CEO) will want to know that their subordinates are doing the right thing.

7.

TOOLS AND TEMPLATES
• • •

THE INDISPENSABLE LETTER OF ENGAGEMENT

The single most important and effective tool a hiring manager or head of executive recruiting can use to improve the value of engaging search firms is a letter of engagement generated by the hiring organization. Among other advantages, use of a standard letter of engagement removes the need to ask the search firm where it stands on a variety of issues; the hiring organization is setting the terms and simply asking for any objections.

The following template has been tweaked many times over the years to reflect the experiences of numerous companies that have used it, and you may want to introduce variations to the following specific terms.

(Company) would like to engage (Search Firm) in a search for (Position). Here are some of our expectations and commitments:

That (Search Firm) will develop, with our assistance, a detailed position specification and a list of organizations where we expect candidates might be found;

That (Search Firm) will communicate details of progress in the search at least once a week beginning in the third week of the search;

That (Search Firm) will document efforts to identify and recruit candidates of all backgrounds, without regard to race, gender, age or other factors unrelated to their ability to perform in the position; further, the search will not be considered successful unless a diverse slate of candidates is presented;

That (Search Firm) will interview finalist candidates in person before presenting them and provide detailed information on each candidate presented;

That (Search Firm) will thoroughly check references and verify all employment and educational credentials for final candidates, as well as agree with the hiring team on who will conduct further background checks, what they will include, and when they will be done;

That candidates presented are not being advanced by (Search Firm) to any other organization;

That discussions with candidates will not include disclosure of information the candidate's employer would consider highly proprietary (such as a customer list or trade secret); and that candidate discussions not include consideration of other employees from the candidate's company who could also be recruited.

That we establish a goal of completing the search within three months, with these target dates:

Date X: Search begins

By date X (within 1st week): We approve the written specification

Week of X (3rd week): Weekly communication begins

Week of X (4th or 5th week): First full review of progress

Weeks of X (5th through 7th weeks): Search firm develops candidates

Weeks of X (6th through 8th weeks): We interview candidates

Weeks of X (9th through 11th weeks): Second interviews for finalists

Week of X (12th week): Offer extended and accepted

If this schedule cannot be met, we expect (Search Firm) to provide notice of each delay and to continue the search until completion, or until we mutually determine that further work is impractical.

We expect (Search Firm) to maintain strict confidentiality on information gained about (Company) and its employees during the engagement.

We expect (Search Firm) to refrain from recruiting any individual from (Company, or a defined unit) for a period of at least one year from the completion of this search.

If the hired executive leaves our organization during his or her first year of employment, we expect (Search Firm) to conduct a subsequent search to replace the candidate at no fee (expenses only).

For our part, we pledge to:

Respond promptly and fully to requests for information and assistance that will help identify and recruit the best candidates available;

Make it a priority to be available for communication, to be prepared and available for candidate interviews on a timely basis, and to provide detailed feedback immediately following interviews;

Pass to (Search Firm) any suggestions of candidates generated through other sources;

Renegotiate the fee if the specification changes during the search to a degree that a substantially new effort is required.

In consideration of services provided, (Company) will pay (Search Firm) a fee fixed at US$xxx,xxx, with one-third of that fee payable upon initiation of the search; one-third 45 days after initiation; and one-third 90 days after initiation. In addition, (Company) will reimburse (Search Firm) for pre-approved travel expenses only. Search Firm will provide an itemized estimate and suggested reimbursement schedule.

If (Company) cancels the search at any time during the first three months, (Company) will pay (Search Firm) a prorated portion of the fee. If (Company) cancels during the first month, one-third of the fee will be considered earned; if (Company) cancels during the second month, two-thirds of the fee will be considered earned; if (Company) cancels during the third month, three-quarters of the fee will be considered earned.

If, within one year, (Company) hires more than one candidate from among those interviewed by the hiring team, (Company) will pay (Search Firm) a fee of 25% of first-year base compensation for each additional candidate hired.

The hiring team will include myself and (name and/or

title). First interviews will be with myself and (name and/or title); second interviews would include myself and (name and/or title) as well as (name and/or title) and (name and/or title). I will make the final hiring decision based on input from you and this group.

We look forward to having (Search Firm) represent (Company) among potential candidates for this key position.

Agreed and accepted:

(Search Firm)　　　　Name, Title, Date, Signature
(Company)　　　　　Name, Title, Date, Signature

A SEARCH FIRM MASTER CONTRACT

If you plan to work with a search firm on a regular basis, you may find it helpful to establish an agreement that covers issues common to all search engagements, including issues of the relationship between the search firm and the hiring organization.

Unfortunately, these contracts normally take in large amounts of legalese in fine print that daunts all but the most determined reader. A more simply worded agreement may be more useful.

Here is a sample contract that can be used along with a letter of engagement for each search:

This is an agreement between (Company) and (Search Firm), effective (date), and expiring (date plus two years).

Termination

(Company) may terminate this agreement at any time with 30 days' notice, with any current engagements to be completed to (Company's) satisfaction unless (Company) is in default.

Termination may occur immediately if either party materially defaults and fails to substantially amend the default within 30 days after written notice, or if either party becomes insolvent.

Confidentiality

Each party agrees that information concerning the other party's business (including affiliates and subcontractors) shall be maintained as confidential and not disclosed, used or duplicated.

Indemnification

(Search Firm) will hold (Company) harmless for any liabilities arising from the relationship, except as caused by gross negligence or willful misconduct.

Non-exclusivity

(Company) does not guarantee a minimum amount of work to (Search Firm) nor does it grant exclusive rights to provide any service.

Fees

Fees will be paid as provided for in Engagement Letters.

Expenses

Expenses will be reimbursed for pre-approved consultant and candidate travel expenses only.

Adherence to standards

(Search Firm) agrees to abide by ethical standards and retained search practices set by the Association of Executive Search and Leadership Consultants (AESC).

Activity reports

(Search Firm) agrees to provide reports on current and past activity for (Company) upon (Company's) request.

Equal opportunity

(Search Firm) will document efforts to identify and recruit candidates of all backgrounds, without regard to race, gender, age, or other factors unrelated to their ability to perform in the position.

Ownership and delivery of research

(Company) retains the right to access, upon request, all information developed by (Search Firm) in the course of performing services.

Offer of position

Only (Company) can offer employment, and (Company) retains the right to reject all candidates.

Extension of services

When successful completion of the engagement does not occur during the projected time frame of the engagement, (Search Firm) agrees to continue to provide services at no additional cost until (Company) determines that the engagement is complete.

Subcontracting

(Search Firm) shall not subcontract any of its obligations

without written approval from (Company).

Off-limits

(Search Firm) agrees not to recruit or solicit employment of (Company) employees during the term of this agreement and for a period of one year following the conclusion of this agreement.

Insurance

(Search Firm) will maintain, at its own expense, coverage for worker's compensation, employer liability, general liability, auto liability, and errors and omissions liability, each in the amount of at least $1 million per occurrence.

Ban on gifts

(Search Firm) will refrain from any gratuity to the company or its representatives for the purpose of obtaining business.

Agreed and accepted:

(Search Firm)   Name, Title, Date, Signature

(Company)   Name,   Title,   Date, Signature

SEARCH OUTCOME REPORT

There's no substitute for writing down what happens in a search and feeding results back into the search firm selection process. Use such criteria to measure internal recruiting effectiveness as well.

Start date:
Close date:
Retained search?   *or*   Opportunistic hire?
Position:
Business unit:
Search consultant:
Firm:
Office:
Number of candidates presented:
Search fee:
Fee as a percentage of compensation:
Search expenses:

Did specification change during search?

Search result:

Outside candidate hired

    Time to present (search start to presentation):

    Time to accepted offer (presentation to acceptance):

    Was search ever on hold?   If so, how long?

    Hired candidate was __ female; __ minority (US only)

Qualified candidates not presented

Offer(s) rejected

Position filled internally

Position filled by referral; search firm not involved

Position eliminated

Other developments made search impractical. (Explain):

Search consultant performance:

 Outstanding

 Good

 Fair

 Unacceptable

Comments: What could be improved?

SEARCH CONSULTANT SCORECARD

In selecting a search consultant, give each consultant under consideration up to 4 points on each of 10 criteria:

Track record here

1 Never engaged

2 Engaged at least once with good results

3 Engaged at least once with great results

4 Engaged several times with great results

Track record elsewhere

1 References reveal no red flags

2 References are positive

3 References are positive, consistent

4 References are positive, consistent, highly relevant

Market knowledge

1 No experience in this particular sector/function

2 Limited experience in this sector/function

3 Solid experience and knowledge

4 Knows "everybody"

Knowledge of us

1 No special insight into our organization

2 Some knowledge and insight

3 Knows and understands our culture

4 Knows us intimately; excels at creating a fit

Access to candidates

1 Significant blockages of individuals and target companies

2 Minor blockages

3 No blockages but not well known to potential candidates

4 No blockages and well known to potential candidates

Diversity

1 Resists diversity requirements

2 Well-intentioned but not focused on diversity

3 Responsive to diversity requirements

4 Excels at recruiting diverse candidates

Capacity

1 Involved in more than 10 searches

2 Conducting more than 5 searches

3 Conducting more than 3 searches

4 Can make our search the top priority

Motivation

1 Will consider serving us

2 Wants to succeed

3 Highly responsive

4 Absolutely determined

Ability to represent us well

1 Sales-y

2 Credible
3 Credible and well-informed
4 Corporate ambassador

Fees and expenses
1 High
2 Reasonable
3 Good value
4 Added value

SCORECARD FOR SEARCH FIRM AND HIRING TEAM PERFORMANCE

SCORECARD - SUMMARY SHEET

Key Data: <Provider Name>

Agreed Terms & Conditions:

Account Manager:	
Name:	
Address:	
Contact details:	
Assistant:	
Placement fee:	
Off-limits guarantee:	
Placement guarantee:	
Off-limits clients:	
Functional expertise:	
Regional coverage:	
Other:	

Assignment History:

Calendar Year	Job Title	Date Closed	Division	Location	Successful placement? (Y/N)	Comment (if not filled)	Cost
202X							
202X+1							

SCORECARD TEMPLATE: OUR ASSESSMENT

SCORECARD - OUR ASSESSMENT

AGENCY & RETAINED SEARCH FIRM SHARED SCORECARD

EVALUATION CRITERIA	METRICS	BELOW EXPECTATIONS	MEETS EXPECTATIONS	ABOVE EXPECTATIONS	CATEGORY WEIGHT	CATEGORY SCORE	TOTAL SCORE
CONTRACT COMPLIANCE					25%	5	1.25
Compliance with contractual obligations	*Actual cost vs. proposed cost	1 2	3	4 5			
	*Sense of urgency (met milestone deliverables)	1 2	3	4 5			
	*Off limits guarantee adhered to	1 2	3	4 5			
Adherence to agreed upon standards	*Replacement guarantee adhered to	1 2	3	4 5			
QUALITY					25%	5	1.25
	*Complete and concise candidate reports	1 2	3	4 5			
	*Profiles matched job description and compensation	1 2	3	4 5			
	*Candidates matched our culture	1 2	3	4 5			
	*Candidate placement success	1 2	3	4 5			
	*Diverse slate of candidates submitted	1 2	3	4 5			
RESEARCH CAPABILITIES					20%	5	1
Strategic market coverage	*Creative sourcing	1 2	3	4 5			
	*Geographic reach	1 2	3	4 5			
	*Effective use of networks & database	1 2	3	4 5			
CUSTOMER SERVICE					10%	5	0.5
Ability to support the service	*Attended weekly update meetings/link-ups and provided regular research status updates	1 2	3	4 5			
	*Proactive follow-up and response	1 2	3	4 5			
	*Proactive resolution of issues	1 2	3	4 5			
BUSINESS RELATIONSHIP					10%	5	0.5
	*Effective Compensation & Benefits support	1 2	3	4 5			
	*Length of time to complete engagement	1 2	3	4 5			
	*Caliber of account manager and team	1 2	3	4 5			
	*Ethical standards	1 2	3	4 5			
	*Support for employment branding	1 2	3	4 5			
Compatibility with our operating culture	*Peripheral services (market information & moves, industry functions)	1 2	3	4 5			
	Candidate assessment, tools and coaching support	1 2	3	4 5			
MARKET BENCHMARKING					10%	5	0.5
	*Search Fee	1 2	3	4 5			
	*Administrative Fee	1 2	3	4 5			
Value of provider relationship (vs market competitor)	*Second placement fee	1 2	3	4 5			
	*Guarantee	1 2	3	4 5			
	*Off-limits guarantee	1 2	3	4 5			
	*Peripheral services	1 2	3	4 5			
OVERALL SCORE							5

Comments:

155

SCORECARD TEMPLATE: PROVIDER ASSESSMENT

SCORECARD - PROVIDER ASSESSMENT

AGENCY & RETAINED SEARCH FIRM SHARED SCORECARD

PROVIDER EVALUATION CRITERIA	METRICS	BELOW EXPECTATIONS	MEETS EXPECTATIONS	ABOVE EXPECTATIONS	CATEGORY WEIGHT	CATEGORY SCORE	TOTAL SCORE
POSITION SPECIFICATIONS							
Quality of specification provided by the company	*Provide a thorough and detailed briefing for each assignment, which will act as the blueprint for the search	1	3	5	20%	5	1
	*Timely approval of final Job Descriptions	2	3	4			
	*Provide clear guidelines on compensation and benefits	2	3	5			
COMMUNICATION							
	*Provide timely feedback regarding the background information provided on candidates	1	2	3	4	5	
	*Schedule candidate interviews promptly and report findings as soon as possible after the interviews	1	2	3	4	5	
Effective communication flow from company to Provider	*Provide information regarding candidates identified internally or from other sources, so that they may be evaluated as part of the search	1	2	3	4	5	20%	5	1
	*Be available to discuss the progress of the search, the challenges in the marketplace, and the steps both parties can take to improve the process, if required	1	2	3	4	5	
EFFICIENCY							
Operating Efficiently	*Provide candidates priority access to senior management scheduling, to move process along	1	2	3	4	5	20%	6	1
	*Timely delivery of offer terms when finalist candidate is identified	1	2	3	4	5	
	*Length of engagement (post-candidate submissions)	1	2	3	4	5	
ACTIVE ENGAGEMENT							
Active engagement of appropriate company personnel throughout the process	*Staffing Partners actively engaged	1	2	3	4	5	20%	5	1
	*HR Managers actively engaged	1	2	3	4	5	
	*Hiring Managers actively engaged	1	2	3	4	5	
PAYMENT							
Payment of invoices	*On-time payment, within contractual payment terms	1	2	3	4	5	20%	5	1
	*Accurate payment	1	2	3	4	5	
OVERALL SCORE							5

Comments:

EXECUTIVE RECRUITMENT SERVICE-LEVEL AGREEMENT

Position Title:	Hiring Manager:
Position Level:	Executive Recruiter:
Date Initiated:	Recruiting Team:

A successful search is typically a result of a close partnership between Hiring Manager (HM) and Executive Recruiter (ER), where both parties are clear on responsibilities and execute crisply on their commitments. This agreement outlines ownership for each area of responsibility and will serve as the roadmap to guide the process and dictate deliverables.

Role	Responsibilities
Hiring Manager (HM)	• Ultimately responsible for hiring decision • Clarify need for position and level • Complete job description • Review and commit to SLA • Accommodate regular search status meetings • Recommend candidate leads or events where candidate might be available. Solicit the same from team. • Identify and brief interview team and executive sponsor • Assign focus areas for each interviewer • Provide feedback on candidates presented within 48 hours of receipt or otherwise negotiated • Reserve time for candidate interviews • Help "court and sell" candidate during interviews • Provide prompt and detailed

- Re-visit and redefine position requirements throughout the search, if necessary.
- Approve final offer
- Engage with candidate after offer is extended to help close
- Drive public relations plan, new hire setup, and on-boarding program
- Participate in post mortem meeting with ER

Executive Recruiter (ER)

- Lead search kick-off meeting
- Oversee development and approval of job description
- Establish search strategy:
  - Choose external search partner or internal team
  - Direct research and sourcing of candidates
  - Present target list and sample profiles
  - Establish "courting and selling" strategy
- Source and screen candidates
- Manage interview process:
  - Present candidates to HM (resume and assessment) with recommendations based on position profile, candidate profile and business requirements
  - Oversee candidate interview scheduling
  - Host candidate for interviews
- Drive communications:
  - Conduct status meetings with HM (weekly preferred)
  - Issue "morning mail" with assigned focus areas
  - Collect interview feedback
  - Provide hire/no-hire recommendation

- Manage offer process:
  - Collect current compensation data on candidate
  - Work with compensation to drive offer recommendation
  - Secure offer approval from Human Resources and HM
  - Extend offer to candidate (verbal and written)
  - Brief hiring manager for follow-up
  - Manage post-offer negotiations
  - Trigger relocation process
- Greet hire on first day
- Confirm onboarding activities
- Conduct "post mortem" meeting with HM

Specifics

The search will commence upon (1) agreement to these terms, and (2) completion of the job description, which will be completed by the HM by _____.

- ER and HM agree to meet for status updates every _____ weeks.
- HM agrees to commit _____ hours per month to review/assess/interview candidates.
- Search strategy will be completed by _____.
- Hiring manager will engage interview team and exec sponsor by _____.
- Estimated search completion date is _____.

Hold/Termination

The HM or ER may terminate the search at any time, with prompt notification and detailed reason. Examples include:

- More than six qualified candidates interviewed with no hire or no decision
- Candidates assessed and rejected based on requirements outside the position specification
- HM or ER not fully engaged on the search (e.g., unresponsive, unable to meet regularly, etc.)
- Altered needs based on changes in group structure from

reorganization, termination, promotion, etc.

Search Post Mortem

A post mortem will be conducted at the conclusion of the search at which time we will review and discuss the process, candidate slate, timeframe and partnership to identify those areas where improvements could have been made. This will help to ensure an excellent experience for future candidates and preserve the Company's reputation for having a professional and respectful hiring process.

POSITION SPEC FOR A SENIOR CORPORATE EXECUTIVE RECRUITER

Purpose

Responsible for the full life-cycle recruiting of senior leadership across the enterprise globally, requiring a high level of complexity related to internal client and external candidate management, assessment skills, and overall search process.

Responsibilities

Conduct searches for the most senior positions in the organization.

Create comprehensive position specifications that support the definition, desired outcomes, critical qualifications, career-pathing, marketing, attraction, and selection of senior-level positions.

Source candidates through referrals, networking, social media, and search research.

Conduct detailed behavior-based interviews with internal and external candidates, providing information on professional background, career progression, alignment to role and organization, compensation, employment restrictions, regulatory licensing, and other required credentials.

Provide consultative advice across all aspects of executive recruiting (intake, attraction strategy, assessment, outcome management, offer, and pre-hire) while establishing trusted relationships.

Meet the organization's hiring needs against specific metrics, including days to fill, search firm utilization versus options, ethnic and gender diversity, offer acceptance ratio, and engagement completion rates.

In collaboration with colleagues, develop the strategic direction of the executive recruiting function. Identify opportunities to increase recruiting effectiveness through awareness of changes in the external executive recruiting industry.

Assist in identifying and evaluating retained search consultants using performance metrics and fit to search needs. Initiate and negotiate master service and statement of work agreements with search providers.

Work effectively with providers of assessment, reference-checking, and relocation services.

Provide spending rationale and/or cost justification for use of recruiting resources.

Create search strategy documents and customized executive hiring reports to identify success factors and barriers to success in leadership recruiting.

Conduct benchmarking data collection for search engagements and new initiative analysis.

Formulate and recommend employment offer packages.

Anticipate and provide critical candidate decision information on all aspects of candidacy, including compensation data and offer scenarios.

Continually develop knowledge of the organization's products, services, infrastructure, and business model as well as that of competitors, which over time creates comprehensive business acumen.

Learn functional roles quickly through effective meetings to assess and make search strategy recommendations.

Participate in the Executive Search Information Exchange (ESIX) and complete required recertification credits to maintain professional designations. Attend additional industry conferences and seminars related to executive search practices and the broader HR function. Build a professional network of colleagues in the executive recruiting space.

Participate in special projects, including process documentation and standardization efforts, HR technology enhancements. learning programs, workforce initiatives (best places to work), and MIM (Metrics in Motion) efforts.

Work effectively with HR Center of Excellence partners, including HR Business Partners, HR Operations, Compensation, and Leadership Development on dependencies related to search assignments.

Demonstrate corporate citizenship by participation in community volunteer programs and diversity programs.

Support broader Talent Attraction functions related to campus recruiting efforts, role-play resources, and external recruitment events. Mentor junior-level recruiting staff.

Qualifications

Bachelor's degree required, advanced degree preferred, HR certification(s) highly preferred.

Minimum 10 years' experience in HR, exempt-level corporate recruiting, or executive search consulting.

Strong business acumen and ability to apply competitive intelligence to candidate selection.

Highly skilled interview and selection capabilities.

Experience with multi-component compensation programs.

Expertise in dealing with and understanding the inner workings of retained search firms.

Demonstrated key competencies including influencing and negotiation, relationship management and partnering, diligence and perseverance, judgment and decision-making, creativity and problem-solving, and organization.

Ability to interact with senior-level candidates through a high-touch approach.

Ability to develop, recommend, and execute recruitment decision rationale to senior management.

Ability to work independently at a consistently high level while managing multiple priorities.

Adherence to guiding principles of trust, ethics, integrity, and confidentiality.

Proficiency with MS Office, process mapping, and search management software.

INDEX
• • •

ABOUT THE AUTHORS
• • •

Simon Mullins and David Lord are the world's leading independent consultants on the management of executive recruiting at organizations of all sizes. It's a narrow field in which their experience runs deep, and their reputations are practically synonymous with the topic.

Simon Mullins has been a recruiter and recruiting leader for almost his entire career—he even started a recruiting agency while a student at university. He has lived and worked in Europe, Asia, and the US (on both coasts), for startups and as a leader at a Fortune 50 company.

Simon has managed executive search from "the outside" as a Partner at Korn Ferry. At Microsoft, he led one of the most advanced internal corporate executive recruiting functions, as well as its largest experienced-hire staffing group.

After beginning his recruiting career in London, Simon moved to Hong Kong to recruit for clients in the technology industry. He joined Korn Ferry in Boston and spent seven years there and in Silicon Valley.

In 2004, Simon joined Microsoft's Executive Recruiting Team, which he led from 2006 to 2012, eventually becoming Senior Director of the company. The team became highly integrated with Microsoft's succession planning process and was responsible for all external hiring of the company's most impactful executives, including board directors.

In 2013, Simon was asked to become Senior Director of Staffing of Microsoft's largest experienced staffing team, serving the Applications and Services Group.

In 2014, Simon joined the Executive Search Information Exchange (ESIX) and now leads and facilitates the group. ESIX (esix.org), funded entirely by hiring organizations, is the world's leading independent information source for corporate executive recruiting leaders.

Simon is a frequent speaker at industry forums and was an ESIX Advisory Board member from 2007 to 2012.

He holds an honors degree in economics and public administration from the University of London.

Find Simon on LinkedIn at https://www.linkedin.com/in/simonmullins/ or write to him at Simon@ESIX.org.

David Lord is a career journalist, having worked as a daily newspaper writer and editor for 10 years and as Editor at Kennedy Information from 1987 to 1995, where he covered the management consulting and executive search industries and became a widely quoted authority on executive recruiting.

In 1995, David formed Executive Search Information Services (ESIS) in response to requests from corporations for better information about executive recruiters and best practices in working with them. Over the next 20 years, he helped more than 100 Fortune 500 corporations improve executive search effectiveness.

In 1996, David created ESIX, a research and discussion group for heads of executive recruiting from leading corporations. Later, he founded the Executive Search Academy, a two-day course in best practices for corporate executive recruiting professionals.

David has served as a moderator, panelist, and presenter at executive search industry conferences worldwide.

He holds a bachelor's degree in psychology from The College of William & Mary.

ACKNOWLEDGMENTS
• • •

It takes a village to raise a book, which, in this case, would not have been possible without the love and support of Simon's wife and business partner, Barbara, along with their children Annie, Izzy and Isaac, and David's wife and business partner, Susan.

We cannot thank enough all the recruiting experts and leaders who have contributed to our learning over the years, including those named in these pages and so many more, and of course especially the current and former members of ESIX.

This book also benefits from the invaluable professional assistance of Carolyn Monaco, Jill Totenberg, Jayme Johnson, Monica Jainschigg and Sherri Dietrich.

WHY ESIX?

The Executive Search Information Exchange (ESIX) delivers research, tools, training and peer networking to heads of executive recruiting at leading organizations worldwide. The group has met more than 400 times and includes most of its original members from 1994, plus 90 more organizations from around the world.

Members attend regular meetings in various business centers in the US, Europe and Asia. They also attend online events on a variety of topics relevant to the recruitment of senior executives.

Participating organizations are entitled to a menu of benefits, including meeting attendance, benchmark surveys, live and on-demand training (at www.ExecutiveSearchAcademy.com), and online tools including the execSmart database of search and research consultants.

ESIX is completely independent, 100% member-focused, and receives no funding from executive search and consulting firms or software vendors.

"I have gained a lot of value out of the relationships and professionally, it has been very rewarding." —Abby Babski, **Boston Consulting Group**

"Great materials!" —Nidhi Hiremath, **BT Group**

"Thanks for keeping us connected during these times." —Jackie Morgan, **Eaton**

"Informative, insightful and delightful." —Eric Goldstein, **IBM**

"I have gained and learned so much out of ESIX and know I will continue to do so." —Kara Buescher, **Kellogg's**

"I have loved partnering with you. You have helped me tremendously in my career." —Toni Unrein, formerly **T-Mobile**

"Truly a fruitful and productive dialogue and information share." —Shannon Pereira, **PepsiCo**

"ESIX membership enabled me to connect with peers to get their help with ways to modernize our executive searches and train my team in a different approach." —Gwendolyn DeFilippi, **US Air Force**

For more, contact Simon@ESIX.org